THE
HANDS-OFF
MANAGER

THE
HANDS-OFF
MANAGER

How to **Mentor People**
and **Allow Them**
to Be Successful

STEVEN CHANDLER
best-selling author of **100 Ways to Motivate Others**
and **DUANE BLACK**

THE HANDS-OFF MANAGER

EDITED AND TYPESET BY KATHRYN HENCHES

Cover design by Wes Youssi

Printed in the U.S.A.

To order this title, please call toll-free 1-800-CAREER-1 (NJ and Canada: 201-848-0310) to order using VISA or MasterCard, or for further information on books from Career Press.

The Career Press, Inc.
220 West Parkway, Unit 12
Pompton Plains, NJ 07444
www.careerpress.com

Library of Congress Cataloging-in-Publication Data

Chandler, Steve, 1944-

The hands-off manager : how to mentor people and allow them to be successful / by Steve Chandler and Duane Black.

p. cm.

Reprint. Originally published in hardback in 2007.

Includes index.

ISBN 978-1-60163-223-4 -- ISBN 978-1-60163-592-1 (ebook) 1. Mentoring in business. 2. Employees--Coaching of. 3. Goal setting in personnel management. 4. Employee motivation. 5. Autonomy (Psychology) I. Black, Duane, 1952- II. Title.

HF5385.C465 2012
658.3'124--dc23

2011045931

To George Addair

So much of what we call management consists of making it difficult for people to work.

—Peter Drucker

ACKNOWLEDGMENTS

From Steve Chandler

I acknowledge Byron Katie for putting me through school and opening up the kindness of the universe that Einstein was puzzling over. Katie's nine-day school was the most transformative experience of my adult life, and I recommend that anyone wondering how to live in peace and harmony check it out at *www.thework.com*.

I acknowledge Duane Black for providing in himself the ultimate role model for successful hands-off management and the full philosophy contained in this book. I also acknowledge him for applying this system so successfully at SunCor and getting the results year after year that verify every concept in this book.

I also acknowledge my wife and hands-on manager, Kathy, for professional and personal rescuing beyond one's wildest expectations. I want to thank Fred Knipe, Steve Hardison, Terry Hill, Lindsay Brady, Michael Bassoff, Ken Wilber, Leonard Cohen, George Martin, Jessica Chandler, Stephanie Chandler, Mar Chandler, and Bobby Chandler, too.

From Duane Black

I have been fortunate to have many people in my life who have made a contribution, but George Addair has likely been the biggest influence on me of anyone I have ever known.

I would also like to acknowledge my friend and coworker Jim Adair, who has been an incredible friend and sounding board for ideas for nearly 30 years. We have worked together for so long that we have become like brothers. Another great friend and discussion partner of many years has been Bill Woodward. Then there are my favorite authors—Jim Carey, Neale Donald Walsch, David Hawkins, and Steve Chandler.

I must also acknowledge my wife and family. They are the ones who love you unconditionally and know you best. They can most easily push the buttons that help show you what judgments remain inside that you still have the opportunity to forgive, release, and let go of.

Duane Black acknowledges that the philosophies, opinions, and management techniques described in this book are his own, and do not necessarily reflect those of SunCor Development Company, its subsidiary or parent corporations, or its leadership team.

C O N T E N T S

P R E F A C E

The secret of happiness lies in the ancient
saying: "Become what you are."

—Alan Watts

In my many years as a corporate trainer and personal success
coach I have never met a leader as quietly powerful and effective
as Duane Black.

The company he works for, SunCor Development, was always extremely successful in creating beautiful, aesthetically
stunning housing communities throughout the southwestern
United States, and the more I got to know Duane, the more I saw
why.

Duane had a way of managing people that was both gentle and impactful. He had a way of inspiring and nurturing success in a totally hands-off, nonjudgmental way. It was amazing to see. Even though he almost never micromanaged anyone, success flourished all around him.

Whenever he would invite me to come in and conduct a workshop for his key leaders, or go to a remote development to work with a sales and administrative team, I would be the one who came away having learned something. I always learned more than I taught.

Duane's practice of enlightened, hands-off management was so fascinating that I would jump at the chance to spend extra time with him. Once he flew me in his Beechcraft Bonanza, a single-engine airplane, to one of his developments in southern Utah. We were talking all the way about his theories of "allowing success" and seeing the greatness in his people.

And the best thing about Duane's theories is that they aren't just theories. They are practices. And they work. Over and over. They work in Utah, they work in Arizona, they work in New Mexico, and they will work anywhere for you.

How do I know they will work for you? Because over the years I have integrated many of them into my own work and teaching. I have taught other leaders and managers Duane's way, and other leaders have benefited and experienced increased productivity when they used these practices and ideas.

They work.

Some of his practices found their way into some of my recent books; some were only hinted at. But now they are all here for you, laid out in ways you can use right away for management and leadership. And the beauty of Duane's practices is that they can be applied to any form of leadership, at home or on the job, in the community or in the workplace.

I spent the better part of a year visiting with Duane at his home on early Sunday mornings, tape-recording his thoughts, discussing his concepts, and listening to his experiences. He and I worked from an outline he had meticulously prepared about his leadership principles and why they function as they do. This book is really his book, and I am very grateful to be along for the ride.

Duane is the one who is there on the job every day as chief operating officer of SunCor, overseeing and managing large numbers of people and projects. SunCor has grown and thrived over the years, and these methods have led the way.

—Steve Chandler

Duane Black lets his people know the deepest truth he knows: All you need to be successful is already in you.

—Steve Chandler

Steve Chandler is generous in his praise and passing along the credit to me for the success of the community development and homebuilding division at SunCor. But he has actually played a greater role in our success than he is taking credit for.

I attended seminars he taught many years ago that helped me form much of my hands-off philosophy and style. His ability to take my concepts and put them into words that bring them to life in numerous seminars and speaking engagements at our company has contributed greatly to our success.

The information in this book, should you choose to apply it, will help you create an organization that functions and performs in a way you never thought possible. Imagine a workplace environment that functions as well or better when you are not there.

You may think this is impossible. You may think that unless you are there to monitor and oversee every aspect of the work being done, it will not be done properly.

But what kind of life does this management style offer you?

If you are the kind of a leader who gets satisfaction from being so needed that your group can't function without you, this book is probably not for you. But if you truly want to create a great independent team, read on. If you want a management system that empowers your people and allows them to grow and prosper, this book will serve you well.

Most managers today are so trapped in daily stressful details that they have no life.

This book was written to give you (and your people) a new life of freedom and real success.

You will find ideas, methods, practices, ways of thinking, and ways of *being* that will allow you to create a team that functions as well without you as it does when you are there.

You can get your life back.

And you can spend your time staying current on market trends. You can fine-tune the way you do business; you can create innovative new services and continuously improve the process in your systems. But mostly, you can become the inspiration behind your team's success.

Ask yourself a simple question: Would you rather inspire your people or control them? Put another way: Would you rather facilitate and guide their success or would you prefer to force the results? You may think force will get you there more quickly, and it may, but it will never withstand the test of time, and your success will likely be short lived.

If you will learn to trust as I have that people already have greatness within them, and that you can help them unlock their potential, they will perform at a level they never imagined.

This has been my experience.

And so now in this book I share that experience with you so that you can learn to see that potential, learn to communicate what you see, and learn to help your people realize and experience the best of who they can be.

—Duane Black

INTRODUCTION

There are three simple words that come to mind when I think of how best to introduce this book, three words that describe the basis of a happy life as well as a successful career: acceptance, love, and freedom. The application of these words also best describes the basis of the hands-off management philosophy of this book.

When one comes from a place of acceptance, one is able to deal with the reality of what is and let go of the misconception of what should be. When one manages others, one simply must deal with who they really are and not who they think they should be. If someone loves analysis and is analytical by nature, why not put them into a role that is aligned with their true gifts? Why try to make them into what they are not? The best managers have quit judging people for what they are not

19

and are focused on how best to utilize the talents they have to serve the organization. They have learned to read people and see where they would best fit in. Employees who do what they are good at don't need a lot of supervision; those who are doing what they are not good at can't get enough supervision.

If you do not love what you do you will never be a real success. You may make money at it, but it will not make you happy. The only real source of happiness comes from serving others and making a difference in the world. And when properly applied, it is also a path to financial success and a life to be proud of. When one is focused on how best to serve one's customer, one naturally attracts more customers. When one is looking to take advantage, they lose customers. Love also applies to your employees. If you do not care about their success, they will not care about yours. People want to be a part of a company that they are proud of, one in which they feel valued and appreciated. That is what will bring you loyalty and people who stay with you even when they are offered more money somewhere else. Love your people and your role in the company and watch success naturally unfold from people who love being at work.

Freedom is so innate and natural to being human that there is a long history of people who have sacrificed their lives to maintain it. Many would choose death over slavery, yet everywhere we look we see work environments that are so encumbered by rules, regulations, and micro-management that they resemble modern-day sweatshops. I am talking about the freedom to be creative, to be unique, to be exceptional, to try something different. We live in a world of ever-increasing pressure to never make a mistake, yet mistakes are happening everywhere we look. Put your people in roles they align with, let them know how much you appreciate them and their good work, and then get out of their way and give them the freedom to be great at being who they are. Watch how they make you successful.

Please read on to discover in more detail how these management concepts can be applied in the workplace to create success beyond anything you have ever imagined possible.

CHAPTER ONE
TAKING YOUR POWER BACK

In everyone's life at some time, our inner fire goes out.
It is then burst into flame by an encounter with another
human being. We should all be thankful for those
people who rekindle the human spirit.

—Albert Schweitzer

Most management activity today is what was alluded to by the Peter Drucker quote at the beginning of this book. Managers make it difficult for their people. They unknowingly kill, or at least diminish, the human spirit by their old-school micromanaging and critical judgments.

But there is a new kind of manager emerging in companies today, a manager devoted to rekindling the human spirit by keeping their hands off their employees and allowing success to happen. We'll just call these enlightened people "hands-off managers."

23

Managers have these two primary communication styles from which to choose:

1. Hands-on: They can criticize, control, threaten, and judge their people.
2. Hands-off: They can mentor, encourage, coach, and genuinely care about their people.

This choice presents itself many times throughout every day. Every interaction with one of your people is going to be a version of this choice.

If you choose judgment (and criticism, implied or otherwise), you will provoke defensiveness and withdrawal—not creativity and productivity.

When we judge our people and find them coming up short, we then start to criticize and micromanage them. In this age of the sensitive, knowledge-based worker, that's a self-destructive cycle. It engenders nothing but resentment and push-back.

Also, when we judge and then hold a grudge, we are giving our power away. When we resent a team member, we are giving our power to that team member. We are giving that power to the very person we are angry with by allowing him or her to occupy and dominate our thinking. We are focused on the problem and not the solution.

Real power in leadership comes from partnering, not criticizing.

The hands-off manager sets himself apart by retaining all his power. His practice is to understand everyone he meets, to see more in his people than they are seeing and to invite them to that vision.

By doing this, he is reducing his own stress level at work. He is completely aware that every time he judges someone he alters his own well-being.

So he refuses to assign the responsibility for negative feelings to the person he is tempted to judge. He assigns the responsibility for these feelings to his beliefs regarding that person.

Only thoughts cause stress; people do not. People cannot.

But for the old-school micromanager the stress never quits, and the harmony in the organization never holds.

If you are micromanaging in the old style of shame and blame, you will recognize this example: You're pulling into the company parking garage and suddenly have to slow down because there's an old person in front of you going slower than molasses. If you then decide you don't like older people who drive slowly, you start to suffer. And you will suffer every time this "happens" to you. Even though it's not really happening to you, it is being caused by you—the stress comes directly from your thought. The older person has no power to stress you out. You think you are suffering because this oldster is driving poorly, but the truth is you are only suffering because of your judgmental thought about him or her.

We all want to be powerful and in control of our own well-being, but we continually give away the very power we seek by our inability to forgive and let go. The only way out of this trap of constant suffering is to cultivate the open-minded, hands-off skills of letting the actions of others roll off our backs and letting other people's negativity go in one ear and out the other.

Anything we cannot let go of has control over us. But once we can let go, we're in control. We can laugh and enjoy how we are unaffected by what other people might be doing.

That's when you change as a manager.

That's when people see you as an island in the storm. A person to go to for peaceful resolutions of crises. In other words, a true hands-off manager who gets results from a relaxed, enthused, and highly productive team.

One does not "manage" people. The task is to lead people. And the goal is to make productive the specific strengths and knowledge of each individual.

—Peter Drucker

How to open your energy field

The hands-off approach allows you to learn to take your power back and live in a world of quiet action and non-judgment. If you do this, you'll soon be living with an open mind, forgiving effortlessly and taking back control of your energy and enthusiasm for doing great work.

Discovering your natural gifts and learning your true nature is not about learning how to force yourself upon your team. It's about allowing success to emerge from within you, and then from inside others. It's an inside job. And once you see that all real power comes from the inside, you can start to become powerful.

There is a story about Wolfgang Amadeus Mozart that illustrates what we mean. A young would-be composer wrote to Mozart, asking advice about how to compose a symphony. Mozart responded that a symphony was a complex and demanding musical form, and that it would be better to start with something simpler. The young man protested: "But Herr Mozart, you wrote symphonies when you were younger than I am now!"

Mozart replied, "Yes, but I never asked how."

Mozart's point was that he simply let the symphonies emerge from within him. He didn't have to figure out how to force something outside him to work.

Duane has a saying he uses at work, although it doesn't apply only to work; it applies to life in general. His saying is, "Find them, don't fix them." It's a policy that encourages finding strengths in your employees that already exist, and allowing those strengths to come forward. It also applies to finding the right people for the job, people whose natural skills and interests align with the work you are asking them to do.

When they do what they love the success will follow. Once you know what they love to do and help them do it, they'll do it for you all day long. Keep finding ways to match their talents with the tasks ahead. Find them, don't fix them.

And there will always be employees for whom you don't find a good job match. Nothing seems to make them happy. Soon, you know in your heart they aren't a fit for the team you have.

Old-school managers have a hard time dealing with this realization. They keep trying to fix things. They keep trying to fix people. They go through endless inept exercises to try to find ways to motivate mismatched employees to get them to do what they really don't want to, and are not interested in or excited about doing. They try to find ways to make them change themselves into someone they are not. This is a waste of everyone's energy!

Our hands-off manager's commitment to finding how our people can fit rather than fixing people who don't fit has been the central factor in the success of teams. Take the case of Barry.

Barry was so stressed by his financial debts at home that he pushed hard for a sales management position early in his employment, and got it. (Barry was very persuasive and a crafty communicator.) However, Barry simply did not enjoy the responsibilities of leadership. He was easily frustrated with salespeople who didn't have his natural love of cold-calling and meeting new people. Even though he tried to learn our principles of coaching success instead of forcing it on people, he was still unhappy, and the results showed it.

We finally identified the mismatch and convinced the CEO, Glenda, not to keep trying to "fix" Barry with leadership training and negative performance reports. We asked that Glenda "find" Barry—the real Barry, the true, natural salesperson wanting (but not being allowed) to emerge.

Finally Glenda saw the light and repositioned Barry as a senior major account salesperson and turned him loose in the field where Barry loved to be. After four months, Barry's commissions were enormous, and he was able to settle all his financial crises at home while loving the job he was doing.

Glenda had just taken her hands off Barry's natural inclination to succeed. And this powerfully effective "find them, don't fix them" approach also applies to us as individuals. We benefit when we continue finding out who we are and letting that discovery manifest in the outside world, rather than trying to fix ourselves.

Learning to turn in a new direction

1. We often enjoy going in person to hear the teachings of a dear friend, a philosopher/guru named George Addair who holds wonderful workshops on personal evolution. (This book is dedicated to him.) One of his sayings is "You never overcome anything." In this Addair means that anything that has been a part of your history will always be a part of your history. You can't make it go away. However, over time, if you choose to, you can simply defuse and dismiss it and go another way. You can follow another path so that the memory loses all its power over you.

2. When leaders are bold and decisive throughout the day, they often make mistakes and bad calls. It's part of being in action. It's a big part of courage. George Patton used to say that an average plan executed right now is far more effective than a great plan that takes a long time to decide to put into action.

3. A hands-off leader can just release a mistake and let go of it. And while it doesn't disappear, it simply becomes old news. It's this letting go of the need to "overcome" things that happened in the past that leads to becoming truly powerful.

4. The Greek word *metanoeo* is translated as "repent' in the English New Testaments, and W.E. Vine's Dictionary states that it means "to perceive afterwards." Therefore, it means to take another look and to change one's mind or purpose, and it always involves a change for the better. So *repent* then means nothing more than "turn and go another way." Some traditions have been trying to teach us that if you've done something wrong, you should punish yourself, feel remorse, and burden yourself with your shameful behavior. What the literal translation really wants you to do is just turn away from it and take a newer, better direction in your thinking.

5. When I reflect on my recovery from addiction years ago I realize I didn't really "overcome" my addiction. I simply took another path. I repented, in the truer, deeper meaning of the word. I realize, too, that if I were to get back on the path of alcohol and drugs I'd have the same problems all over again. The code is there in my brain for addictive drinking. So if I started drinking again, it would be addictive. And it doesn't matter whether the code came from repetitive use or genetics; it's there, so I just don't go there. The process is to not go there. To replace the false spirit of drugs with true spirit.

6. I know from my personal experience that "overcoming" truly doesn't work. It doesn't have any track record of working in the workplace, either. And when you hear people who are newly happy with their jobs now, they say, "I've moved on. I've just moved on." They don't say, "Well, I was able to come to grips with it, wrestle with it, overcome it, conquer it, defeat it." No one who is truly free of a problem such as addiction says, "I was able to overcome, defeat my alcoholism, and it lies in a heap and I am victorious over it." They just say, "I've moved on. I've accepted my powerlessness and taken another path. It's not a part of my life. I've chosen a different way, a different form of spirit than alcohol."

7. Carl Jung said, "People do not solve their psychological problems, in my experience. They outgrow them. They grow in a different direction and just leave them in their history." This is what the process of allowing success is all about. It's the heart and soul of hands-off management. It's considered a revolutionary form of management because it breaks the old codes of manipulation and mistrust.

8. Some therapists say that in order to move on, you must re-enact a conversation you had with your antagonist all over again and resolve that memory that's inside you. But that's just giving more strength to the story. And we are looking to free you from your stories. Micromanagers in the workplace do the same dysfunctional thing those therapists do. They relive

breakdowns and mistakes and go over and over them, making people wrong all day long.

Why not just leave it there and move on? Release its power over you. See it in a different light so that you can focus on your natural talents, your God-given gifts, and bring the best of who you are to the surface.

The hands-off manager uses this principle to not carry grudges; he meets every person in the workplace with equal trust and understanding. The past is merely something you have learned from. The mistakes were a blessing, because you now know how to do it better going forward.

Most micromanagers in old-school organizations today immediately think that when things go awry, they have to overcome them. They imagine a Rambo figure who can overcome any odds and can fight off 50 or 100 people at a time if he has to, because he is so strong in his ability to overcome. Our national macho mythology nurtures an image of a guy who is really muscular and adept at fighting. So we build into our culture and collective psyches the idea that "If I only became stronger, if I only worked out harder, if I only ran more miles, or went to more seminars, or pushed myself harder, then I'd finally become strong enough to deal with the issues my team is facing."

But the opposite is true. If you want a strong mind, you must learn to quiet your mind. If you want real power, you must learn to let go. Greatness exists within everyone, and your biggest job is to get out of its way and let it come through.

Doing this will eventually make you incredibly powerful. Not so strong that you can lift hundreds of pounds at one time, but strong in a different, deeper way. So strong that you can discipline your mind and discipline your thoughts to let go of anything that isn't serving you. So strong that your people draw their strength and calm from you—just from being with you! You don't have to say anything for them to feel how peacefully powerful you are. They warm up to your vision, and teamwork begins to emerge of its own accord. It's being inspired to happen instead of forced to happen.

No more team-building seminars

Companies often ask me for a seminar in team-building. I don't give them anymore. I know that if people are not performing and communicating with team spirit, it's not a team-building issue, it's a leadership issue.

I am very direct with the manager asking for the training. I want her to see that great leadership will create a culture in which teamwork will simply grow. They don't need team-work training. The manager herself needs hands-off leadership training so she can learn to mentor success instead of trying to impose productivity.

If you are a newly enlightened manager you have begun with a shift in awareness. You've pulled your power back from the external world of form to the internal world of energy. You now know how to shift your awareness up and over the bothersome event so that you can see another more productive path to take.

You cannot be attacked from this lofty position. Even if people say negative things about you, you don't end up giving your power to them. You keep it in yourself. "Negative" occurrences don't bother you so much anymore because you simply use them for practice. You actually gain strength from them.

Is it a tough discipline? Yes! It may be even harder than working out with weights. Because it's so counterintuitive at first. It goes against our whole upbringing and training.

Learning the inner game

When you study people in history who knew the secret of inner allowing versus outer overcoming, you find that they usually had long, happy lives. Bernard Baruch, who died in 1965 at the age of 95, was an American financier, stock market and commodities speculator, statesman, and presidential adviser.

After his success in business, he devoted his time to advising a range of American presidents, including Woodrow Wilson and John F. Kennedy, on economic matters for more than 40 years. Baruch was highly regarded as an elder statesman. He was a man of immense charm who enjoyed a larger-than-life reputation that matched his considerable fortune. Baruch is remembered as one of the most powerful men of the early 20th century.

When asked about his long life and success, Bernard Baruch said he discovered the key when he was younger. He said, "In the last analysis, our only freedom is the freedom to discipline ourselves."

What? Ourselves? Not overcoming outside obstacles?

Here is another way to look at the hands-off manager's shift in inner awareness. Imagine going to the airport with a huge suitcase. You don't even consider trying to take it onto the plane with you because you know it won't fit or be allowed. So you check your bag and let the airline take care of it.

But what if you tried to board a plane the same way you try to live your life?

You'd be carrying all your heavy, inappropriate, disallowed baggage onto the plane! All your hurts and resentments and tiny betrayals get carried around with you. Imagine going through the airport and picking up other bags, not even your own, and trying to carry all of them onto the plane with you! Your spouse's baggage, your kids' baggage, and all your direct reports' baggage.

Is there even enough room on this plane?

This may sound like a slapstick comedy, but it's how many of us who play micromanagement roles in society live today. Just keep this in mind: If you did this with your baggage in an airport, you would not be allowed to fly.

And the same is true with your career. By trying to carry all this baggage (by trying to remember who has done you wrong, whom you don't trust, who disappointed you, what department you don't get along with), you are too burdened to fly.

Take your hands off your life to allow success and allow yourself to fly.

Allowing your career to take flight

When my son Bobby was a little boy he was always asking me about various sports figures and superheroes.

"Dad, who would win in a fight between Arnold and Bruce Lee?"

"Bruce Lee."

"Who would win in a fight between Superman and Batman?"

"Superman."

"What if Arnold and Superman fought Rocky, Chuck Norris, and Spider-Man?"

"Okay, time for bed!"

We are actually fascinated by questions such as these, which is why such fictional heroes as Rambo and Superman endure. And the internal power that can lift you up through your organization is more akin to the power Superman has than the external power Rambo tries impose on events. Rambo is a human being who can be brought down by a bullet. And if he were shot in the heart, he'd die; there'd be no more Rambo. But one of Superman's abilities enables things to bounce off of him. He has a power beyond that of Rambo. If someone fires a bullet, he just pushes it away with his hand and moves on; it doesn't affect who Superman is. That's why his archetype calls to us. That's why he endures and speaks to the inner hero in children and adults.

He has the power to deflect rather than overcome.

You can shift your whole way of leadership thinking. You can shift your awareness to be totally in tune with what's happening with others, and what's happening with you. And whenever you see something come up that doesn't align with you, you don't fix it; you accept it, deal with it, deflect it, and move in a newer, healthier direction.

Deepak Chopra once wrote that when you get "bad news," it becomes good news if you suspend judgment. It was always good news anyway. It was just in disguise. "If you don't get what you expected, look at what you got," says Chopra. "Where is the gift in what you received? Is there a way you can transform it into an opportunity to learn? In this approach, change is accepted, not denied. A sense of spaciousness enters in."

The spaciousness he describes is exactly the shift in awareness we are talking about. It's a shift from narrow, judgmental, constricted awareness to a bigger, more spacious, hands-off allowing.

Chopra concludes, "On a profound level, every event in life has two possible causes. Either what happens is positive, or it is bringing up something you need to learn in order to create something positive. It's the same with the body. What happens inside a cell is either healthy activity or a sign that a correction is needed. Although life can seem random, in fact everything is pointing to a greater good. Evolution is not a win-lose crapshoot, but a win-win journey to transformation."

You'll learn your true nature this way, by being free from the effects of everyone else's nature. It's a way of giving yourself space, of giving yourself the freedom to live out your true professional potential, to discover what's possible for you!

Because once you have gotten rid of all of this limitation, weakness, anger, and sadness, you're back into possibility. You're enthusiastic once again about ideas and innovation and the very things that move this organization forward. You are truly focused on solutions. Problems are just the process that allowed you to perfect your path.

Soon you'll have a different definition of personal power. You'll realize that if you are truly powerful, you can let go. You can forgive. You can release. You can deflect. That's the real power.

Greatness is within you. There is nowhere you need to look to find it. It is already inside, waiting for permission to express itself. If you knew you already had something, why would you go looking for it? The trick is to remember. Remember to let go of all the negative ways of thinking that are obstacles toxic to your success. Remember to allow your success to take its natural course and happen for you. The success you find will be greater than you ever imagined possible.

Steps to hands-off success in your life

Three action steps to take after reading this chapter:

1. The next time you feel a conflict with someone, write down two things you appreciate and admire about that person and sit down to resolve the conflict by telling them these things first.

2. Take mental and physical notes about everyone who works with you so that you become more and more aware of each person's loves and strengths. Start a notebook about this, and don't forget to include yourself in it.

3. Begin noticing your own thinking throughout the day as you lead and communicate: Which thoughts bring you down? Which thoughts lift you up? By practicing this step you will begin to understand that it is always your thinking that creates your feelings, never other people.

CHAPTER TWO
REDEFINING SUCCESS FOR YOURSELF

To laugh often and much; to win the respect of intelligent people and the affection of children...to leave the world a better place...to know even one life has breathed easier because you have lived. This is to have succeeded.

—Ralph Waldo Emerson

Your first job as a hands-off manager is to manage your inner life. It is impossible to mentor others toward success if you haven't done it within yourself. Hands-off management begins at home in the mind of the mentor.

So how do we make sure we become successful? Most people never succeed, because their definition of success always includes some change in the outer world, and the outer world is so hard to change. So you might begin by redefining success for yourself. And you might find that the definition itself is already inside you—not in some book or audio recording.

Sometimes you'll read or hear something that seems profound. It feels as though it could make a difference and shift your awareness about how life could work for you. But you also have a funny feeling about it. You may be thinking, *This is something I already knew.* If you are reading a book and a certain paragraph rings true, you may underline it to read it again. Then you get that familiar feeling again: *This is something I already knew.*

This is a sign that your life's purpose is already inside you! You don't have to seek it out. If you had no awareness of what your life's purpose was, how would you have known that those words could apply to you? If you didn't have an innate and natural understanding of your potential, how would you have been touched by those words?

When a group of people are reading the same thing, they'll each respond to different passages differently. Reading groups always experience that. People think it's because they just have different tastes and preferences, and they don't think beyond that. They don't realize that what calls to them from the book is resonating with something already inside them. It's the energy, spirit, and force that's within communicating: What you've just read aligns with who you are.

Once you wake up to this inner resonance, you will know when things have meaning for you and how you can use them in a way that will benefit your life.

This inner tuning and intuition is at the heart of hands-off management. You don't need to get your hands on the world to shape and manipulate what's already perfect inside you.

You can even go one step beyond that if you're open to it: You can realize, "If I can recognize it by reading it in a book, then I'm not learning it from the book, I am being reminded of it by the book. And if I'm being reminded of it, it must already exist someplace inside me."

So if it already exists, would it not be possible without the reading and without the external exercise, to just let it come through?

That's the key to a hands-off life: Find a way to let the best of what's in you naturally come through.

Rather than racing around learning all kinds of new managerial systems, procedures, and trendy formulae, you just get better at knowing yourself and the person you are managing. You'll then learn how to let go of your old ideas. You'll learn how to find what's already there, rather than going looking for what you think you're missing. Napoleon Hill said, "Think and grow rich." But we are saying, "Remember and grow rich."

When you manage yourself and someone else it is only the negative thoughts you have that get in your way. If you believe negative, limiting thoughts about yourself and the other person, then those thoughts will manifest in the outcomes you experience.

Radical? Contrary? Let's start here: Think about how you use your mind. Why do most of your ideas, inspiration, concepts, and solutions come to you when you're singing in the shower? Or when you're just relaxed and being quiet? Or when you're driving down the road not really thinking about anything?

Many surveys and almost all anecdotal inquiry show that managers get their best ideas in the shower, when doing easy yard work, or while on vacation. Why is that?

It's because you've stopped trying to control your thinking. You've taken your hands off your mind and allowed the wisdom within to emerge.

It always will.

At a mental level, this is similar to the difference between talking and listening. People have taught for years that if you listen, you will learn more than if you were talking. But people have always assumed that "listening" only means listening to another person, an all-too-narrow interpretation of the word. Hands-off management starts with listening to yourself, tuning in to your own heart and mind, because if you will learn to listen to your inner being, you will learn more than when you're always trying to talk to yourself about how things should be.

Most of your thoughts are created by fear. Have you ever noticed that? Especially if you believe them without question. They are centered on your survival as a manager, so they are worried thoughts, scanning the future for possible problems and catastrophes. You function as a human scanner all day long. The problem with that approach is that it leads to hands-on micromanaging. It leads to trying to manipulate your people out there in the external world. It also leads to a life of worrying about your own future, and therefore a life of always feeling anxious and distracted.

The people you're dealing with may feel as though you aren't there. And you feel it, too. It is the very definition of stress. It is the very source of workplace fatigue and burnout.

To try to get relief from all this anxiety, a micromanager will often dip back into the past. But that's not much better, is it? When you're in the past you are spending the majority of your time thinking about what you feel guilty about. Shift to the future and you're back to what you're afraid of. How can you mentor someone from that sort of "bipolar" mood swing? How can you be present to the task at hand and the person in front of you?

To truly mentor someone you must be at peace. When you are not at peace the other person will be contaminated by your stress. So find the peaceful place inside you that tells you what success really is. Then go forth and model the same peaceful efficiency and creativity to others. That's the beauty of hands-off management in a nutshell.

True success is less about reaching the final goal and more about using each moment to make progress toward the goal. Focus more on how you can be constantly moving forward and what the next step is. It will make the ultimate goal that much easier to achieve.

Steps to hands-off success in your life

Three action steps to take after reading this chapter:

1. Make a list of all the external, material goals you have in your life. Then ask yourself about each object (a car, a boat, a vacation home): Why do you want it? How will it feel to have it? Write that feeling down as the true goal, with an openness to the possibility that the feeling can be achieved without (or prior to) achieving the material goal.

2. Write down your financial definition of success. Give it `a number. What does success mean to you financially? Then ask yourself why you want the money. For what purpose? What feeling do you want that you don't have now? A feeling of security? A feeling of power and freedom? When you've written it down, allow yourself to be open to the possibility that you can have that inner feeling without (or prior to) receiving the money in your life. Then open yourself to the possibility that wealth may even flow faster into your life when you are at peace and feeling secure, powerful, and free.

3. Write down your relationship and family goals. Why do you want these things? How much of what you have written down depends on other people acting in certain ways?

Then rewrite them focused only on what you want to contribute to others regardless of how they behave, or their "loyalty" to or "appreciation" of you. Make these goals within your capacity to reach now, right now, and not at some future time when the world corrects itself.

CHAPTER THREE
USING THE POWER OF NEUTRAL

Balance is the perfect state of still water. Let that be our model.
It remains quiet within and is not disturbed on the surface.

—Confucius

Kerry was a division leader obsessed with creating a new incentive plan for her major telemarketing teams. This obsession was causing her anxiety and stress.

All her focus in the past had been on negatives. She wanted certain guarantees that her people would not betray her. She resented certain past behaviors that she was now trying to eliminate. The more she fretted, the more she micromanaged, and every time she tried to negotiate a new plan there was a war between the two sides. She couldn't see that she was creating the war. She was creating havoc every time her irritated voice proposed a new plan.

I met with Kerry for a coaching session prior to yet another meeting she was about to have with her top people.

"I'm worried about this meeting," Kerry said.

"Why?"

"I know they'll argue against this plan and ask for more guaranteed salary, which I don't want to give them because they will all get lazy on me if they don't have to work for commissions."

"You don't trust them."

"They haven't earned it."

"People have to earn your trust?"

"Of course. I've been burned too many times not to know that."

"I'm not surprised that you've been burned so many times."

"Really? Why?"

"You don't trust your people."

Kerry was silent. She said nothing.

I took more time in the coaching session than normal because I wanted to introduce Kerry to a new concept called hands-off management. I wanted to teach her what I'd learned from Duane Black—that if she didn't trust her people it was because she didn't trust herself. Her entire mind was filled up every day with stressful thoughts about worst-case scenarios. No wonder she was struggling and filled with anger.

Her first step in the journey from hands-on to hands-off would be to meet with her people for two hours with no agenda on her side of the table.

"No agenda?" asked Kerry. "You can't have a meeting with no agenda. We learned that in our leadership training."

"Right. And that training was first developed in the 1940s for companies run on the old-school military model of management. It counted on a workplace of people hoping for 30 years of loyal service and a pocket watch at the retirement dinner at the Holiday Inn."

"What would I look like, having no agenda?"

"Someone who cared what their lives were like as telemarketers. Someone who wanted to listen, someone who was neutral about how this final arrangement would look."

"Neutral?"

"Neutral."

It took Kerry a full year of coaching to make the trip from micromanaging to mentoring. A full year of internal reprogramming. But she did it. It was a great year for her and her self-esteem as a leader. And listen to her today, in her words from a recent e-mail:

It's funny how much I look forward to work every day. It's such an adventure not knowing. I'm so happy to explore and open up in new ways every day. There's no rigid way I have to be anymore, because I'm no longer obsessed with doing it right. Or not getting in trouble. I think our society does that to little girls. Little girls fear getting in trouble. Making daddy mad. Little boys are given more leeway. Boys will be boys! They get to fail a lot and make tons of mistakes growing up. Girls better get it right the first time! You've showed me that as true as that scenario might have felt in my past, it's just a story now. I can cling to the story or let it go.

What I like most about the past is that it's over.

—Byron Katie

Organizational life is a constant process of negotiation and sales. It's an ongoing opportunity to promote a particular perspective in order to accomplish a purpose you are working toward.

There's no way around it: You're always selling.

Whether it's selling ideas to your team, a concept to your own supervisors, or a new service to a customer, your day is spent selling. As the author Robert Louis Stevenson said, "Everyone lives by selling something."

But not everyone sells the same way.

Not everyone sells from the same position. In fact, what really sets a hands-off manager apart is the position that Kerry learned to take: neutral. Managerial mastery is simply an unusual mastery of the neutral position.

Not positive, not negative, but neutral.

"If you and I were negotiating a land acquisition structure, my strategy, my way of being, would be not to resist anything that you bring to the table," Duane says, "it would be to accept it, to acknowledge you for having brought up that issue and then to focus our mutual attention on the benefit of the position that I came to sell in the first place. And that way, you have an invitation to shift your position. If I resist your position, then my challenge to you is to defend it, not look at an alternative to it. Because we can't operate completely outside ego; it wouldn't be human. We each have a little bit of a tendency to want to defend whatever position we have taken."

Reality dances best with someone who is flexible. Success flows toward an open (neutral) position. The best negotiators have an open, neutral mind—not a closed mind.

Sales and negotiations will occur internally, too—inside one mind at war with itself.

We were communicating with a friend this morning who's a professional golfer, and he was having such a hard time getting into tournaments and doing well, even though he's a great golfer, because negative thoughts keep coming into his mind as he's about to hit the ball. Throughout his career he's been trying to force them out and force positive thoughts into their place.

What I recommended was that he step back from both positive and negative thoughts to what he might call a neutral position. Simply observe the thoughts, let them pass by, and then hit the ball with nothing in mind whatsoever. Not by forcing a positive: *I can do this, it'll be great, it'll go in.* And not by being worried: *Oh no, I'm going to blow this.* But to just step back and allow thoughts to pass like clouds. And when there's an opening, hit the ball. From neutral.

Everything improved. "Neutral" is powerful.

Learning negotiation from physics

As I sat in Duane's study early on a warm Arizona Sunday morning discussing the amazing power of neutral, he told me that he deepened his understanding of its power by observing the structure of the atom.

In atomic structure there are always three forces: there's an electron, which produces a negative force; there's a proton, which produces a positive force; and there's a neutron, which remains neutral. The neutron and the proton create the nucleus of the atom, and the electron travels around that nucleus at very high speeds. Electricity is a function of the negative electrons transferring through a conductor from one atom to the next. So the negative is very elastic; it's very moveable throughout all of physics. A negative force moves easily from one place to another.

On the other hand, the neutral force and the positive force are much less moveable. When you separate the nucleus—the neutron and the proton—you unleash violent atomic energy; that was the basis of the atomic bomb.

"So that connection," says Duane, "that bond, in my opinion, which is based on physics, simple physics and chemistry, has been proven to be where the real strength is in business. The connection between the positive and the neutral. Although the negative has to be there to sustain balance, it's very easily swayed and moved and transferred to another atom. In the case of human beings that means to another person, with little effort. We're almost too open to it. But you can't, without a severe response, separate the neutral and the positive."

That brings us back to the hands-off manager's respect for neutral observation as the ultimate vision. As a true and artful observer, one must be without judgment and without a position. A true observer gains power from seeing all valid positions from a neutral spot.

Those of us who are managers deal every day with opposites. We deal with up and down, success and failure, hard and easy, fast and slow, happy and sad. What we don't always understand is that those opposites go together and need each other. We can only experience easy because hard exists. We can only experience up because down exists.

Yet we're always anxious to remove the opposite of the experience we seek! In reality, it's impossible. The experience we seek could not exist in a relative universe (and workplace) where everything is understandable only because its opposite also exists.

So a worried, fussy micromanager's resistance to opposition, and to the opposite of that which he seeks, blocks him from getting to where he was trying to go. He gets good critical feedback, and instead of being open to it he's immediately defensive.

He ends up more worried about the negative he wants to get away from than the positive he wants to move toward. And ultimately he can't get to success from there. The "there" he is stuck in has too much worry to gain traction and move.

The hands-off negotiator has power

The real power is pure neutrality, in any aspect of negotiation.

When you want to achieve "good," you can't get there by resistance to evil. When you want to achieve "right," you can't get there by resistance to wrong.

You win by realizing that hot and cold are the same thing—they're just opposite ends of temperature. Win and lose are essentially the same thing—they're just opposite ends of the experience of the game. In and out are the same thing—they're just opposite ends of movement within or movement without.

In a good negotiation, you'll learn to give up the resistance and the judgment of the opposite of that which you seek. You'll accept the opposite and incorporate it into your own position.

But neutral means neutral. You just don't care if no deal is made. You're not striving for one of those frantic, win-lose deals in which you give away the farm in your desperation for success.

People who do that don't realize that attaching to a certain outcome pushes that outcome away.

Remember, neutral is the attractive force. (They called it "playing hard to get" in high school.) The neutral position is always the most effective.

Once you become neutral, positive and negative then become the balancing forces. When you are neutral, you're automatically attached to the positive, if you look at it from a nuclear physics perspective. The negative is brought in to create the balance, but the link between the neutral and the positive is where the power lies.

The problem is that we don't accept that. We keep trying to make the negative go away.

But that's akin to trying to iron the waves in the ocean to make the ocean smooth. Or cutting the positive pole off a bar magnet so that you just have the negative.

Futile.

The balance of all three forces reflects the nature of life. But in order to get the positive, most managers go out and fight against the negative, and wonder why more negative keeps coming in.

We do this trying to manage our society, too. We hire more police to oppose gangs, and wonder why we have even more gangs. We create more government programs to fight poverty, and wonder why poverty continues to grow. The very things we fight against become the things our attention goes into and empowers. What we resist persists. What we oppose grows stronger. Consider that your attention is the fuel of change. What you pay attention to is the fire that you are adding fuel too. If you truly want a positive outcome, focus on the solution and not the problem.

There are other ways to deal with gangs and poverty that address the whole, balanced system instead of just addressing what's "wrong" with the current system.

New solutions show up as whole systems.

What you resist will always persist

A gifted chiropractor we know (we'll call her Judy Smith) became a corporate business consultant, and she was terrified that she would have no credibility with clients because of her limited background in business. She feared being perceived as a "mere" chiropractor. Because she was so focused on getting rid of the negative (her perceived lack of credibility), she took the technical doctorate she had earned as a chiropractor and put it on her business cards and Website. She was now "Dr. Judy Smith." Clients just assumed she must be a PhD in organizational development, which was what she hoped would happen.

But it didn't take long for the word to get out that the "Dr." Judy was using was for being a chiropractor, and she was made fun of. The very negative she was trying to avoid came back at her in a bigger, more vicious form. What she opposed grew stronger, and what she resisted persisted.

Later she stopped resisting, and told clients up front about her successful chiropractic practice. She dropped the "Dr." from her name. She told wonderful stories about her work as a chiropractor and the lessons she learned that she could apply in creative ways to business. People loved it. So by not resisting reality, reality became her ally. By no longer feeling negative about her former profession, she could return to a powerful neutral position.

In the workplace, the old-school micromanager is obsessed with eliminating the negative. And by doing so, he himself becomes negative, judgmental, and non-trusting, focusing only on problems (thereby making them bigger than they are). Ignorance of neutrality leads managers into a world of deception, dispute, and control. None of those attitudes is an aspect of neutrality.

This is why managers who are controlling and micromanagerial get so much push-back from their people. Their people feel paranoid and judged.

But when they give up dragon-slaying the negative, managers become hands-off managers. And from that place without judgment, they can focus their attention on that which they wish to create. What a relief to everyone.

In every person, even in such as appear most reckless, there is an inherent desire to attain balance.

—Jakob Wassermann

Alan Watts used to say that his definition of the human ego was "defense of a position." That is exactly what the workplace ego is: defending your isolated position in the organization. But when you fight for a position instead of embracing the entire system, you contract your being into something small and weak.

The bigger part of you is the part of you that is unconditional, accepting, and without judgment. Many just don't grasp that that's the really powerful part of you.

The power aspect of neutrality is that it allows you to be an observer who is open to all possibilities. When you meet with team members from another department you can hear their side of the story and see whole-system solutions. You are not overly defensive of your position in the universe.

In negotiations, neutrality is a mutually inclusive concept that most businesses now acknowledge is the only real way to do business if you want longevity and a lasting network of relationships with the people with whom you negotiate. The old macho idea of besting your "opponent" in a negotiation gives people a short-term thrill and a long-term headache. Professional athletes whose agents best the team to get multi-million-dollar contracts often earn the scorn of fans when they have a bad year and leave the sport in shame and disgrace.

Neutrality brings you to honest solutions, and, most of all, it lets you allow—not force—the results to move toward a fruitful outcome.

Author and social scientist David Hawkins talks about surrender being the most powerful path to enlightenment. And in today's world of the macho, Rambo-like computer-game character, people almost cannot conceive of such a thing being the path to power.

But ironically it is what martial-arts hero Bruce Lee taught. At only 135 pounds, Bruce Lee was, pound for pound, the strongest fighter on the planet. No one could defeat him—not even the biggest American boxers, with whom he did exhibitions. He once said, "To be a great martial artist, you become water. Water is totally accepting of whatever gets thrown into it." And the big American boxers would lose because they would punch outward and try to defeat who was in front of them. Bruce Lee said, "I'm like water and you are jumping into my ocean when you fight me. And to be like water is the most powerful way you can be, both as a martial artist and as a human being."

Water is soft and accepting, yet it has the power to level a city.

Bruce Lee said the only American boxer who came close to that principle was Mohammed Ali, because Mohammed Ali would dance and "float like a butterfly." And with his amazingly flexible body, he would invite his opponents' punches throughout the fight in such a way that they would punch themselves out, being drawn like moths into the neutral fire Ali was embodying. And by the time an opponent was so weary he couldn't hold his arms up anymore, Mohammed Ali would jump in and finish his fight. He would "sting like a bee." But he never actively resisted his opponent early in a fight. Nonresistance was his neutral, successful position.

Former Secretary of State Dr. Henry Kissinger was one of the greatest negotiators of all time because no one could come up with a position that would offend him. No one could upset him. No one could put him on the defensive. He was always willing to understand the other side's position, so they could almost always find a whole-system solution that would in some way work for both of them.

Duane Black has been a master negotiator for land acquisitions for many years. He says, "When you're negotiating with someone and you find things that they have to have, that they just can't live without, you can get so much in return on your side of the equation by giving them those things, it's amazing. And that happens a lot. Sometimes people will have a particular hot button, and if they can get that, they'll give you everything else."

A skilled hands-off negotiator never has to make a deal happen. He never gets so attached to a particular outcome that he can't move to the idea of higher opportunity. He can always push back from the table and say, "Gee, I would have loved for this to work but I can see it's probably not going to work in a way that will serve both of us, so I'm happy to just take a step back."

Back to neutral, the position with all power. Back to where it doesn't matter if it "works out."

"And it will amaze you how people will respond to that power," says Duane. "How people are drawn to the fact that you might want them but you don't need them."

Remember high school? The most interesting young women seemed to prefer the guys who could take them or leave them. And the needy guys who were desperate to have them, who couldn't live without them? The young women didn't want anything to do with them.

As human beings, we're not attracted to needy relationships. We don't want to be involved with someone who needs us desperately. Needy feels creepy, which is why stalking is a crime.

The other person's neediness takes a part of us away. It becomes a mechanism of control, and we don't want to be controlled. We want to be free. That's our very nature.

The neutral perspective allows the best possible outcome for both parties to emerge. There's no forcing. And even though you're always drawing attention back to the benefits of the direction you would prefer to see things go, you're also open-minded. If the other side has a new idea about a different direction that you hadn't thought of, you can shift right along with it. Smoothly, without resistance. Because you have no position to defend. You're not attached to any particular outcome, except for the higher good.

That's the power of hands-off neutrality.

Steps to hands-off success in your life

Three action steps to take after reading this chapter:

1. The next time you are negotiating with someone in the workplace, give yourself time in advance to enter the world of "neutral."

2. Actually write down all the good things that might come from this negotiation not resulting in a "win" for you. Get comfortable with the "worst thing that can happen" so that you lose all sense of needing this to go a certain way.

3. Schedule three meetings with people in your organization with whom you have not had the easiest time talking (people you don't like). Then have a no-agenda meeting with each of them in which your position on everything will be neutral. No position. You will be there to listen and learn and be taught by the greatest teachers you will ever have. The people you like are not your best teachers, and by valuing neutrality, you'll learn this.

CHAPTER FOUR
USING FOCUS AND INTENTION

The universe always gives you more of what you are focusing on.

—Alan Cohen

I met with Kyle in his penthouse office overlooking Atlanta and encountered his litany of stressful thoughts about the future. Kyle thought they were legitimate concerns about the present.

"The list is endless," he said. "I've got so much to do today that I sometimes feel like jumping out of this window."

"That's one option," I said. "As long as you don't do it while I'm sitting here. That would be my request of you. As your coach."

"Well, what would you do?"

"I'd go on vacation."

Kyle laughed bitterly. That was the last thing he could possibly do with all these crises coming up.

57

I said, "Kyle, will you do an exercise with me right now? I think it might help us sort this out."

"Sure. Whatever."

"Close your eyes and let your mind travel back in time to the last time you felt happy when you got out of bed. When was the last time you felt total peace inside, and started your day in a fully relaxed and happy way?"

Kyle took a while. Finally he said, with his eyes still closed, "My trip to Mazatlan. I remember waking up each morning with nothing to do. We didn't plan much on that trip. We just woke up whenever we wanted and walked to the patio and looked out over the water. It was like being in heaven."

"And so you did nothing?"

"Oh no! We did a lot of fun things. Our days were full. But it was funny that there was no stress. No real need to be anywhere. We just did whatever came to us."

"So you did a lot."

"Quite a lot and it was all fun."

"Did you have lists of what to do?"

"No. We had ideas, even before we went there. But we just did things as they occurred to us. One thing at a time."

"And so I think you've hit on it, Kyle."

"What? Move to Mazatlan?"

"In a way."

"What do you mean?"

"You said it. You gave yourself the answer."

"What did I say?"

"You said you did one thing at a time."

Using Focus and Intention

Kyle thought for a moment. Then he said, "Well that's not possible around here."

"Really? What were you doing before I came in?"

"I was finishing up the Bertoia Report. In fact, I sent it off as an attachment as you were walking in."

"So that was the one thing you were doing?"

"Well, yeah."

"Try to see that all your life you have only done one thing at a time. It's all you ever have to do. It's all you've ever done. It's always worked for you. It always will. You just don't trust it, so your mind races into the future and you try to do 100 things—in your mind—all at once, and that's what causes you stress."

Kyle and I talked for a long time about the impossibility of doing more than you can handle. That coaching session was the first in a series that moved Kyle away from his worried to-do list of 100 action items he was staring at all day. He soon learned to take his hands off that massive to-do list completely and keep it in a drawer. Kyle soon adopted his Mazatlan lifestyle of "one thing at a time." That's all he would ever do, and all he would ever have to do. He learned to live at work just as he did in Mazatlan, doing one happy, relaxed thing at a time, and learning, to his surprise, that it would always be more than enough to bring him success. Kyle learned to live in the present moment.

You can see how old-school managers such as Kyle are so painfully attached to all these things they *have* to do all day (which are, in reality, nothing but thoughts).

Managers similar to Kyle would look at the list of 100 and be repelled by very the sight of it! They'd shrink away in fear. So they would do something else. Something not even on their list! Out of fear of not being busy.

What could these struggling managers be focused on instead of that grim list? They could be focused on their intention to make progress in the present moment. The present moment is the only place where one's life can be moved forward.

That's where all creativity occurs, when it occurs.

True power—the real measure of actual power—is your capacity to create results in this moment, right now.

> Effective managers do first things first
> and they do one thing at a time.
>
> —Peter Drucker

Hands-off management means hands off the past and hands off the future. Your focus is the present moment, because you understand that productivity always happens now.

Then, as your people also learn to create freely in the present moment, success, rather amazingly (and simply), comes to them. When we are in that creating mode, we are advancing upward, evolving and expanding toward higher levels of success.

Creating always occurs in the moment. Never in the future.

When our minds are in the future we experience thoughts of worry and fear. When we drift back to the past, thoughts of regret or resentment arise.

Are any of those thoughts worthy of clinging to?

Allowing success requires nonattachment to such thoughts.

Attaching to your thoughts like Velcro

Professional writers get something they call "writer's block" when they start believing their thoughts about the future.

Attachment to those thoughts allows no room for freedom and creativity.

This habit of attaching, like Velcro, to every passing worried thought and every little judgment leads us into a life of emotional teeter-tottering all day long. A life of fearful distractions.

Sit down with an unsuccessful (unhappy, struggling) manager and you will hear him describe where his focus goes: "I get too many phone calls. I have too many personal problems to deal with. My health is not ideal right now. The person down the hall has their internet gaming site on. I have too many visitors. I'll never be able to answer all my e-mails. My reports are overdue. I have too many meetings to attend this week. I have to give a talk."

Notice all those stressful thoughts crowding in on him. The hands-off manager learns to take just one of those thoughts ("I get too many phone calls") and work with it ("I'm putting my calls direct to message. I look forward to hearing them later when I'm ready and focused on them").

Hands-off managers are creators. They take one stressful situation at a time and create something good from it. Hands-on managers, on the other hand, are reactors. They react to all thoughts, all day, full alarm. For them, life itself is just a series of emergencies.

We lift ourselves up from that when we become creators. When we speak of God in religious terms, we often call Him (or that force), "the creator." Which is why Deepak Chopra humorously says, "God is my role model." He wants to live in the image of his creator by creating. Whether we know it or not, as we go through life, we all ultimately seek and desire an increased capacity to create. To create fulfillment, happiness, and the ultimate in professional satisfaction. What we all want, what's a part of our very core, is that capacity to create. And we lose that capacity whenever we lose focus.

As the great teacher of human consciousness Byron Katie says, "If you want to be unhappy, get yourself a future."

If we wish to move toward a particular outcome, we have to do something right now to create that movement. We can't move something in the future. And we certainly can't undo anything in the past. We only advance when we are in the present moment. Only that sacred place will give us room in which to work.

Why should we all use our creative power? Because there is nothing that makes people so generous, joyful, lively, bold, and compassionate, so indifferent to fighting and the accumulation of objects and money.

—Brenda Ueland

Don't focus on what you fear

In business you begin to realize you can never solve a problem by thinking about it in the same negative mood that created the problem in the first place. You can only solve a problem by focusing on it with a higher state of consciousness. Or to put it more simply: You get yourself into a better mood.

When you become a hands-off manager you are always aware that resisting the things you don't want contributes to their power. Therefore, if you tell an employee he is doing a bad job, you are sowing the seeds of future bad work. For example, if you tell an employee with a drug addiction problem that they're a terrible person, they will feel bad and want to go get another fix. But if you tell them they have potential, that they can learn from what they've gone through, if they can find a way to recognize it as something that was positive, you're able to invite them to a new place of pure recovery.

Old-school managers worry a lot

Old-school managers manage by worrying. They believe that if they don't get worried enough about something, they won't solve the problem. So their internal motivation system is fear. They think they have to scare themselves into doing the right thing.

If you tell them they would be more effective as relaxed, happy, hands-off managers, they tell you they're afraid that if they try that approach, everything will fall apart. They think that without fear as the ultimate motivator, no one would work—including themselves. So they use fear to motivate themselves and intimidation to motivate their employees. They continue to fasten their minds onto the very things that block them from making progress. They're never focused on what they can do right now to move things forward.

If they are in sales, for example, they're not thinking about who is on their referral list or what kind of follow-up calls they might want to make, even though those present-moment activities would move success forward. Instead, they're obsessed with whatever frustrates them the most. If you ask them how it's going, they'll spew out a list of their most current frustrations, which are always at the top of their mind.

A compassionate hands-off sales manager will rectify that situation. He will teach his people to use their "now" moments creatively. They'll familiarize themselves with the products they're selling. They will spend time studying to develop their skills. If they're selling homes to people in their community, they will learn about local community events and activities.

All of these things are ways of focusing attention on what you can do now.

Some surveys show the average salesperson spends only 1.5 hours a day selling. That's because of his focus on distractions and things he considers to be threatening. But salespeople who transform from failure to success have simply realized that walking forward (by living in the now) is much more advantageous than walking backward (by living in the past) or spending their time worrying about what might happen (by living in the future).

Salespeople who struggle are taking one good step forward (identifying an intention) and then two nightmarish steps back (trying to make all the "bad" things in life go away). They wonder why they daily have that uneasy feeling of always losing ground. (They are.)

When you are a manager focused in the moment, you are moving your team forward again. You are paying attention to what's being communicated to you. You are honoring every experience. You are finding value in everything that has ever happened to you. You have respect and caring for others. And it's a different kind of caring. It's not, "I care what you think about me," but rather, "I care enough for you to want you to just be who you are. I accept you, I don't want to fix you, I just want to understand you as you are and partner with you, moving forward in agreement."

Many people think being focused in this neutral, accepting way would make them passive and directionless managers. Quite the opposite! Pure action emerges from an undistracted mind. It's a clear mind that gives birth to the most beautiful quantum leaps of inspired action and bold, creative communications. Because that is where intention enters the picture, rises up, and takes over. It's important to have intention. But intention is different from an outcome goal, and knowing the difference is vital to your success.

The goals of companies and individuals striving for success are often expressed this way: "This goal represents where I want to go, and I'm going to be really unhappy and disappointed if I don't arrive there. This is what I expect of myself, and if I don't get there I will be a failure."

Obviously this kind of thinking only introduces stress into the human system. It builds discomfort and unwanted pressure. Stress is not optimal for performance. This has been proven over and over in everything from free-throw shooting to spelling bees: Stress and anxiety have a profoundly negative impact on performance.

That's why it's more effective to use peaceful inner intention. One can more easily think, *Well, that's where I intended to go, but, oh well, I didn't get there.* It may sound weak, but it's actually stronger, because from that relaxed place you are more likely to keep trying. You are able to say to yourself, *Gee, it was just an intention, it's okay that I didn't get there. I'm going to keep working on it. I've got great new ideas.* Instead of: *I'm disappointed and angry with myself; I'm a loser, I can't progress, and I can't make it.*

With intention you can be like the water Bruce Lee spoke about. Being like water, you allow your nature and your energy to flow along with your intention. With a stressful goal you're always trying to push yourself uphill to finally "get to" the goal. But with an intention, there's no place to get to. No hill to climb. The intention is in you already. You already have it. You just flow with it and use it as a directional monitor.

At its core, intention is a powerful place to come from inside you, and a goal is a hoped-for place outside of you to get to. The truly successful person has learned to get his or her hands off of future outcomes and just flow like a river.

Steps to hands-off success in your life

Three action steps to take after reading this chapter:

1. Rather than focusing on large, external goals that stress you out, keep your task list simple. List three action items you think are the most important to do today and then pick just one to do right now.

2. Once your first three priority items are finished (one at a time), you'll feel a real glow inside, and you can turn to page two where you have other action items listed. Circle one more and do that immediately.

3. The next time you talk to someone, take time to really be there. Don't multitask, check your smart phone, or think of other things. Just be in that conversation and create the relationship you are in. Slow down to the speed of life. Who you are right now is more important than some future visionary quest you're obsessing about.

CHAPTER FIVE
QUESTIONS LEADING TO SUCCESS

Judge others by their questions rather than by their answers.

—Voltaire

The hands-off manager doesn't spend a lot of time giving advice.

Instead, he perfects his ability to ask questions. Questions that allow success and fulfillment to happen. Questions such as, "What things come naturally to you? How comfortable are you doing this work? How easy is the workflow for you right now?"

We have been trained by the media, by our families, by our traditions, and by our culture to focus on the negative and try to fix it. We obsess over sins and shortcomings, trials and tribulations. We try to go outside ourselves to change the negative things. Then we try in vain to create an external situation that's positive.

But none of that works, because the positive solution is on the inside. What we were seeking was already in us. No wonder we couldn't find it out there.

And just how do you find these solutions inside you? Questions! Just start asking questions. And then listen. Take just a moment after you do something and question how it feels to you. You just sent an e-mail to a team member whose actions upset you. Do you feel a sense of satisfaction? Do you feel a sense of fulfillment? Could you say to someone, "I loved doing that. That was fun for me." Or do you feel a sense of guilt and dissatisfaction?

Just listen to that feeling, whatever it is. With a little practice and discipline, it's not hard to find a way to test all your actions against this inner knowing. To tune your instrument for excellence and efficiency. Soon your e-mails and other communications will be both compassionate and powerful. You will tune in to ways of communicating that are clear and satisfying.

I was talking to a manager named George about slowing down and listening to his inner, higher wisdom, when he finally said, "You mean I should love everything I do?"

"That would be ideal."

"If I wanted to do that, all I would do is play golf!"

Very funny, George. But golf is your entertainment, not your work. And entertainment has its place in our world. But unless you're a pro sports figure or an actor (and even those people work very hard at accomplishing what they do), entertainment will not bring you true joy and fulfillment. It will not give you a sense of satisfaction and well-being. Those kinds of feelings only come from what you accomplish, what you contribute, or what you do to make a difference.

Your work will provide you these feelings. Your true feeling of success will only come from what you give to the world through your work and love, while entertainment is based on what you can get from the world.

Jack Nicolaus worked incredibly hard on his golf game, and he actually gave a lot. A professional sports figure, he had millions of people follow him and gain pleasure from watching him play. That's what he was getting paid for. So his level of play was a gift to sports fans.

He also worked at golf in a different way than we do. We just go out and play at golf, but it wasn't play for him. It was a discipline, and he was only at his best when he transcended the play. The difference between Jack's golf and our golf is that Jack's golf was a gift to someone else, and our golf is only entertainment for ourselves. Giving versus getting—one of the deepest principles of hands-off professional success.

The ultimate functional question is this: "How can I contribute?" or, "What can I give?"

Most people in the workplace are focused on *getting*. They want to get instant results from their efforts. They are obsessed about the external and the negative. They fret about how much time off the guy next to them takes, and how much more pay the other person gets, and how much more time the other person spends on personal conversations. Their self-criticism turns outward all day.

But then there's a happier, more successful person in the workplace who is living inside a different mindset. A different set of questions, such as, "How can I do a better job? How can I contribute? How can I make a difference here? What can I do to make this a better company?"

That darned person! She just keeps getting further and further ahead of the negative person next to her! The judgmental person next to her continues to become more and more resentful of her success. And for the life of him Mr. Judgmental cannot see what is causing Ms. Happy's success—which is living with a different set of questions.

Success comes from the questions you ask yourself.

When negative people try to figure out other people's success, they ask all the wrong questions. They ask, "Were they the first ones to work that morning and the last ones to leave?" Or, "Did they make sure they didn't make a single personal call that day?" Or, "Did they make sure they didn't take any breaks or greet people, visit people, and catch up in the break room?" Or, "Did they avoid making mistakes?"

They don't realize that the success occurred because that person came to contribute. Not to compare. Not to worry about what she was going to get. She came to give. It's amazing how the ones who don't worry about what they're going to get are the ones who always seem to get the good stuff. And those who come to get something wonder why they can't obtain it! They wonder why life always feels so unfair. Those who come to give something wonder why they always receive a raise without even having to ask for one. They wonder why they're the ones who are always considered for the promotion, when others have been there longer.

It's fundamentally a shift from trying to force success to happen, to allowing success to occur through continuous contribution.

The hands-off manager models, inspires, and nurtures this giving approach. He or she mentors contribution. When you take your hands off people's lives and let them give what they've got, you'll be allowing them to succeed. They will look to see what's inside them and figure out how they can give that to the world. And that is what allows them to be successful. They don't have to strive for it anymore. They don't have to force it. They don't have to use rigorous willpower. They just have to do what they love to do. Soon they will always be thinking about how they can share their natural ability with those they serve.

To know what you prefer, instead of humbly saying "Amen" to what the world tells you to prefer, is to have kept your soul alive.

—Robert Louis Stevenson

Leigh was trying to trust this practice of contributing by doing what she loved to do, but she had a hard time making it fit into her lifelong negative belief system.

"I just have a hard time trusting that life will bring it back to me," she said over coffee in the break room. "I don't know, I'm having a hard time trusting life."

So Leigh doesn't want to give of herself completely until she can trust that it will be worth it. She doesn't yet see that she has it backward: the giving comes first. Just do your job in an excellent way. Don't worry. Be too busy to worry.

Soon, with mentoring from her hands-off manager, she started giving anyway. A year later she was talking differently.

"Life will give back to you whether you trust it or not," Leigh said. "Life doesn't require my approval or trust. It just delivers the way it does."

Leigh learned that life doesn't always give you what you want—life gives you what you believe. You can only see what you believe is there. The more you trust the process, the more you can stop worrying about what you are going to get back and just give, trusting the process of life where you know one way or the other, you get back what you have been giving out.

If you believe one of your employees is lazy, you can only see a lazy employee, and even if he takes extra time to perfect a report he's writing, you see the extra time as procrastination, laziness, and failure to complete his work. This judgment gets in the way of his greatness and your ability to enjoy the potential that's really there.

Sometimes a new manager will take over an old team and the productivity soars. Why? It's because she didn't believe anything negative about the new team. Instead she met with each team member and asked the questions, "What can this person contribute? Where is the particular greatness in this person? What does this person love to do?"

Steps to hands-off success in your life

Three action steps to take after reading this chapter:

1. Meet with yourself. Ask yourself what your gifts are and how you can best contribute to the overall good of the mission.
2. Meet with each person on your team. Take a lot of time with each to talk about his or her gifts. Some won't think they have any, but you'll find them by asking what they most love to do. Those are their gifts.
3. See the whole team as a beautifully harmonized network of contribution. Draw a map of your team on paper with a big circle for each employee, with their gifts written inside and lines of contribution connecting them to each other, other departments, and your customers. A giving system. Sit back and look at your paper and let it sink in: You are there to keep their channels of contribution (the lines on your paper) open and flowing freely. As a manager that's your primary job.

CHAPTER SIX
INSPIRED IDEAS LEAD TO SUCCESS

So long as new ideas are created,
sales will continue to reach new highs.

—Dorothea Brande

Surveys of successful businesspeople who are asked the question, "When do you get your best business ideas?" keep yielding the same two answers: number one, in the shower; number two, on vacation. This helps prove the point that the best ideas come when you stop forcing your thinking. The straining involved with forced thinking is actually pushing ideas away. You are repelling that great idea wanting to just float up and announce itself. The solution is to gets your hands off your thinking process and let inspiration flow to you.

Once you learn to do this with yourself you can do it with your people. You can plant seeds and ask questions which they can then take away and contemplate. Don't demand immediate answers. Don't micromanage problems. Once you truly see the unlimited potential of your people and the limitless possibilities that life has made available for them, you won't have to worry about how to think of good ideas. You'll just let them roll in.

"So maybe we should take showers and go on vacation all the time!" a small-business owner said after looking at one of these surveys.

He was not far from the real answer; our best practice will be to get into that relaxed, hands-off state of mind that occurs in the shower and on vacation. The real answer is to learn to listen and recognize, to learn to be available for the ideas that are in us instead of trying to find them in a manual or guideline.

That's the secret discipline involved with success. It's in allowing yourself to step back and let it happen. It's a tough discipline to learn at the outset, but it's a rewarding one. It rewards you in large ways by helping a great career unfold. But it also rewards you in smaller, more immediate ways, too: For example, you can actually finish your workday with a low level of stress. You can learn what it means to do less and achieve more.

But I thought you had to think to grow rich

People keep trying to succeed through forced thinking because they've drawn a false conclusion about it. They spend all day thinking about something, and when that doesn't get them the answer, they finally just stop thinking. But then, boom! Once they stop thinking, they get their brilliant idea!

And then they credit the thinking. They don't see that it was the stopping and relaxing that delivered the idea.

Here's another example of how this works. Someone will ask you someone's name and you know you have it on the tip of your tongue. But in the moment they ask you, you can't remember it. Try as you might, you can't think of it! You keep forcing your mind to produce, and it just won't. But a few minutes later, when you're talking about something else completely off the subject, the name will come to you.

That's the way of the mind. And that's the way the hands-off manager uses it. Successful ideas will come to you once you learn to trust that process.

To put it another way, the fundamental key to success now becomes self-trust and belief in yourself. Belief that you've already got everything you need inside you.

That's not an egotistical point of view, because it's not coming from an "I'm better than you" orientation. Instead, it comes from "I have this life in me just as you do, and I'm trusting this life. Therefore success is coming through me. You can do the same thing!"

When you become successful, others notice. They notice that you use a hands-off approach with yourself. You don't worry yourself to death. You don't stress out over deadlines. You don't try to seek the approval of others. You don't try to anticipate what others think of you. You don't use fear as your personal motivator.

Soon your example of fearless success becomes an invitation to others, not a basis of comparison to show them where their weaknesses are.

Talking the other day to a manager about his inner talent prompted him to say, "Well, you know, you've coached me in this over the years, and I'd like to believe you, but you're masterful at it. I don't really think I could do what you do. You've got a unique personality."

What a laugh! But when you are a mentor who has become successful you will encounter this quite often. People will want to put you on a pedestal because they assume your position is due to the strength of your personality—a personality they think they just don't have. This is your perfect opportunity to set them straight and get them on board. You might say to that doubting person, "Remember that analysis you did for me on that difficult property two years ago? Man, that was a good job. And remember that outline you prepared for me on the land plan for that project? That was incredible. You have such a gift. If only you could believe that the same gift that you exhibited on that exercise is also possible from you in what you're trying to do now. Imagine what you could accomplish."

The hands-off manager sets the stage for success by always taking employees back to their own personal experiences of success. When encouraging them to believe in their own greatness, you can't make it theoretical. You have to take them back to something they have done that they're proud of and that they were acknowledged for. Remind them of how they made a difference, and point out to them the skill set they have already exhibited. This factual evidence is what nurtures the self-belief in them that you want.

It's amazing how many people can shift to higher levels of success once they are mentored this way.

One company leader was skeptical and asked, "Isn't your approach to management a little soft? I mean, if all my managers become hands-off, how can I drive performance and hold people accountable?"

But this is not a soft or passive approach. Our experience shows increases in energy and productivity when a hands-off approach is used. It holds people *more* accountable for high performance, not less. It is not patient with people whining and playing victim. It has no room for self-pitying complaints.

And sometimes a hands-off manager can be "hard" on team players to wake them up to their power. You do want to get their attention. So you might say, "Look, this is ridiculous. You're one of the most talented guys I've ever worked with. I've watched you perform at a level that was truly exceptional. And now you're stumbling over this? This is not acceptable. It shouldn't be acceptable to you, either. Clearly, judging by what you've done in the past, you can do this. And now you're thinking of excuses as to why you can't? That's not going to work. Step up and do what you've already proven you have the ability to do. Tell me what I can do to assist you right now."

When do you take the harder, tough-love line? When you are inspired to do so. It will just occur to you, and you'll follow your inner prompting.

If you deliberately plan on being less than you are capable of being, then I warn you that you'll be unhappy for the rest of your life.

—Abraham Maslow

Here's the inspired idea from which all other ideas flow: A successful life exists in everyone. It's not something you have to go search for in the outside world. We are born to be functional and fulfilled. Everything we need has been given to us (including the ability to add whatever else we want to add): We don't have to go search for how to breathe. We don't search for how to see or how to hear. We just accept that they're a part of what we have inside of us. Success is in there, too. It's programmed from birth because it's the way of the universe. Evolution is inevitable and just the way things work. Why would it not include personal and financial evolution?

Your innate instinct exists for all the things that will make you successful. All you really need to do is challenge the false concepts that convinced you otherwise. By virtue of the very reason that you can breathe, you have life. And life means potential, potential to be better and better in your work.

Surprisingly, many people resist this simple truth.

Martin was a classic example. He had become a masterful skeptic. When he was told that he already had it in him to be successful he said, "Look, I've tried to go there in the past and I've been disappointed."

Martin then recounted how some New Age spiritual version of "trusting life" through mythological symbols was ultimately disappointing. He'd been to seminars that got him high and then he crashed. Martin had this experience confused with what we were asking of him: to go to life itself, not somebody else's version of "how life was meant to be," but your life right here, right now.

And even though people claim to have been disappointed from trying to follow a conceptual version of this, they're not disappointed when they do a real-life version. The real-life version works.

Disappointment and mismatches

The world has laid out a false description for us of what it means to be successful. Most of the books you'll read that define success associate it with becoming an admired leader, becoming financially abundant, finding an ideal partner or spouse, or living for a long, long time. But those pursuits are all comparison-based in their definition of success. They focus as much on one-upping or excluding others as they do on inner peace and happiness.

In the hands-off understanding of allowing success, it's useful to find a more inspired idea of success. Most people who are open to inspiration arrive right here in the present moment. And their "success" becomes doing what they love right here, right now.

Of all the false gods of success, wealth has to be the worst. Of all the least inspired ideas, extreme money-making is king. And most people who are wealthy will tell you, "Yes, I'm considered successful. But I'm not happy. I have a real missing piece in my life. I feel an emptiness. I feel a craving for more."

An extremely "successful," very rich man we know was recently asked, "You have hundreds of millions of dollars. Why do you keep working so hard? How much money is enough?"

He replied, "I don't know. But I know it's always more than what I now have."

That's what success becomes when you make success about attaining or acquiring something outside of you. You're always racing toward an unattainable, frustrating, just-out-of-reach future. How widespread is this futility? Pull up a chair in a sidewalk café in any major city and watch the people rush by. Hurrying away from the present moment trying to get to their own futures.

Whenever people make success be about "how much" or "how often," they can never have enough. Because no matter where they arrive, they feel there's still more to be accomplished. That's why managers who use money as a motivator never get the great results they want. And it puzzles them.

Working with Angela, who runs a small business in Boston, we would often hear her say, "I don't get why Janet isn't producing for me. I keep adding incentives and potential bonuses to her sales plans and she still never achieves her plan. Do you think I should put her back on a base salary, or should I make it more commission-based to raise her fear of failure up to where it can finally really serve me?"

Most hands-on micromanagers are focused on money this way. Fear is a motivation they understand. But it leads to frustration, low productivity, and turnover. The human system can only take so much fear before it cuts and runs.

But what if success simply became the process of growing? The same sense of growth a flower feels as it reaches for the sun? Here you are in this moment: improving, evolving, and progressing. How does that feel?

What if success were nothing more than the satisfaction you get right now from doing a little better than you did yesterday?

As you learn hands-off management, you can return your future-addicted people to the present moment. You can show them that being in the here and now is not hard to do. It's returning their focus to the one thing they are doing instead of "all the things I have to do to this week." It's taking them out of feeling swamped and overwhelmed and returning them to a time-management system that has them doing only one thing. Their consciousness is now being used to see what they can do to merely take the next step. It's not straining to see what life will be like when they have finished everything or when they have more and more money in the bank. It's helping them see what they can do to move forward one more step right now, in this moment, today.

That's the hands-off approach to managing life: Don't do everything; just do the one good thing that's next.

The only difference between a problem and a solution
is that people understand the solution.

—Dorothea Brande

Laurel was rushing off from work to a night class when she said, "I don't know why I'm taking these classes. I'm searching, I guess. I read everything I can get my hands on. I don't know what I'll do for a living in the long run, but I'm going to keep looking for it. And I'm going to keep studying, and I'm going to read all the books until I find it."

Laurel would be better off sitting alone in a dark and quiet room all by herself. As Pascal famously said, "All men's miseries derive from not being able to sit in a quiet room alone." Notice that he said "all." Not some miseries. All.

Why doesn't Laurel see that she's chasing something that's already in her? Because the chasing keeps her from seeing. Try looking quietly into your own heart while you're running across the street. All Laurel really has to do is sit in a quiet room alone. And sooner or later she will ask her innermost being, "What would I love to do?"

People often say, "I'd love to go on vacation," because it's a place where they can let go of the chasing. It's a place where they can stop attaching and adhering to their stressful thinking—where they can stop judging themselves, where they can close the door on self-critique and just relax and enjoy the moment and be entertained by life.

The hands-off manager wants that "vacation mind" in the workplace. A workplace where you can incorporate relaxing and enjoying yourself, and allow what's natural in you to come through.

But wouldn't that slow down productivity? Not at all; in fact, our experience has shown that the opposite is true.

Steps to hands-off success in your life

Three action steps to take after reading this chapter:

1. The next time you take a shower, stay in a little longer than normal just to observe how easily ideas are flowing to you from your right brain into your left. Relax in the warm harmonic of the water and the sensation that you are taking your own sweet time. Let yourself notice the connection between relaxation and letting go, and inspired ideas.

2. Have a meeting with a key player on your team and bring no agenda to the meeting. Simply ask her how life is going for her right now, how she's feeling about her work, and what she sees as possible improvements in the work area. Let ideas rise to the surface.

3. Change the way you manage your time. Have only one item on your to-do list. Make the top page your to-do list for just today, and leave only one thing on it. Have the second page contain all the other tasks you used to think you had to do, and when you finish your one thing—doing it thoroughly, slowly, and well—put another task from the possibility list on your fresh to-do list. Just one thing.

CHAPTER SEVEN
Practice Finding an Inner Vision

You will recognize your own path when you come upon it,
because you will suddenly have all the energy and
imagination you will ever need.

—Jerry Gillies

We were working with Jack and Melissa, a husband and wife team of business owners who had just suffered the pain of trying to train an incompetent employee for four months to no avail.

It took them all four months to realize they were not going to succeed. They were trying to force their new hire into being able to do her job as a division leader. The problem was that the new hire hated the work and was constantly making absent-minded mistakes. She didn't have the skills and talents necessary to do the job.

83

We asked Jack and Melissa about the hiring interview.

"We had a bad gut feeling," said Jack. "But her resume looked so good and her references were great. And we needed that position filled so badly. I guess we were hoping for too much. Letting our wishes get in the way of good judgment."

"But Jack, it wasn't good judgment you were ignoring. Good judgment said to hire her based on the resume and references. You were ignoring something else. Something more valuable than good judgment."

"What was that?"

"How you felt about her. Your instinct. The voice inside. It was trying to tell you she wouldn't work out and you didn't listen."

Learning to make your decisions based on this kind of inner listening is different from trying to judge what the "right" or "wrong" thing to do would be. That's the old school of management—to take "right and wrong," make them absolutes, and try to impose them on the workplace. Just because almost every manager does this doesn't mean it works. It seldom ever works.

Go deeper. Find what you are aligned with and what feels natural to you. With every decision you think you have to "make." (Actually, for the hands-off manager, decisions have a way of making themselves, of becoming such obvious choices that no real decision is necessary. You just instinctively know what to do next.)

Interview a candidate using your inner listening and you'll know if he or she is a fit.

Then, as you bring people onto your team, you'll become skillful at choosing the people with whom you feel a sense of alignment. You'll know them. You'll feel a sense of wellbeing when you're around them.

Now it's time to do the same thing with your thoughts. Don't try to ignore or overcome any negative thoughts. You don't have to make thoughts wrong, because that's focusing your thinking on them all the more! Just notice the thoughts that produce the bad feelings, notice their lack of validity, challenge their truth, and then turn and go another way.

Picture two paths opening in front of you. One is the path of alignment; one is the path of misalignment. One is the path of what feels good for you; the other is the path of what feels "off" to you. Not "right" and "wrong" for the world; we're just talking about you, now.

If you spend your time thinking about where you don't want to go, then that path will call to you. And then you'll be frustrated because that's where you end up. And now you can see why.

Some top leaders say a great leader is a visionary. And we know they are referring to market trends, product and service development, and all the things business magazines tell them to talk and think about. Visions of the future.

The hands-off manager is a different kind of visionary. The hands-off manager's vision is not a vision for what the company will be in 10 years. It's a vision that sees the potential of his people right here and now.

Your success as a hands-off manager will be directly related to your ever-increasing ability to see more in your people than they're seeing in themselves.

The next step is inviting them to your vision of their potential.

When you are allowing success (by keeping your hands off of its natural flow) you redefine success as loving the act of making progress. You and your team love making improvements, gently raising the bar, and then enjoying the next step in the journey. Your key skill becomes a relaxed, compassionate observation of what flows and what does not.

This vision goes other places, too. For example, you acquire a new vision of the customer. It's a gentle obsession with customer observation. Because you realize that if you don't observe your customers and figure out why they're buying or not buying, you will lose your ability to help them. Once again, vision becomes observation. It's not a fantasy trip to an island in the future. It's now. It's here. Your customers are just waiting to tell you how to relate to them.

And so it is with the people on your team. If you don't observe your people and how they're feeling, you won't be able to notice their natural skills and abilities. A good hands-off manager is similar to a sports coach who spends time studying the last game's film footage to observe how his people performed, to see how they moved and what their natural abilities were. The coach may even observe how to use those players differently in the next game.

It's the same process of observation in the work arena. You make an invitation for your players to enter your vision of their talent, and then you coach them into enjoying the process. Do just that and you will see amazing results.

In the end, successful leadership has very little to do with power and control. And it has nothing to do with catching mistakes and writing new rules. That has the opposite effect of allowing success.

If the workplace is to really flow to success, you must have the fewest rules possible. You want the rules that you do have to be the minimum to comply with regulations, and that's it. Why? Because you value the unrestricted. You value open-mindedness and creativity. You want to nurture and mentor your people's love of what they do. And that comes through best in an environment not bogged down with rules. We are creatures who naturally love freedom. We do our best when we are unrestricted. When our mind is free to create, not when we are constantly worried about compliance with the latest set of rules.

When we believe in this life and its limitless nature we become more limitless ourselves. The market and the workplace each become a microcosm of that wonderful sense of life.

When we stop thinking about our limitations we start being open to possibilities. We get out of our own way and let prosperity happen. And that, in itself, becomes our discipline.

Discipline?

Yes, the hands-off manager believes in discipline and practice. Because we're deprogramming and unlearning a very big portion of what we've been taught all our lives, it's more an undoing than a doing, and it is a discipline. The whole history of management has taught you the opposite of the hands-off approach. So it takes practice to undo all of that. And the most difficult part of this practice is to alter your belief about what your experience has taught you. That may sound odd. But consider this: life brings you what you believe, not what you want. Therefore experience, which is something that is generally tied to an external event, is merely the reflection of what you've been believing.

The more rapid the rate of change, the more dangerous
it is to live mechanically, relying on routines of belief
and behavior that may be irrelevant or obsolete.

—Nathaniel Branden

For most people in the old management systems, their experience is a reflection of their belief in limitations and disappointing performances.

But just because you haven't done something well in the past doesn't have to be an indication that you can't do it well in the future. It may just be that you never believed in yourself. You never believed you had the ability. Even though you loved to do it, you never believed you were capable of it.

So step one is to first find your management style in what you love to do. Step two is to allow yourself to believe that a new way of successfully managing people is possible for you. Step three is to attach to only those thoughts that come to you that reinforce that belief. (The other thoughts will challenge you, but if you keep at it they will dissipate.) Take those three steps and you will get there.

Then teach it to your people.

Sound too easy? Still, most people will not want to do this. They will think of all the reasons why they can't, and so they won't. And that will simply be more proof and more evidence for them that life does not work out, thus confirming and reinforcing their belief.

The joy of hands-off decision-making

The discipline of being a visionary leader consists in learning to choose. But not choosing the positive over the negative—that's the old-school approach, which doesn't go deep enough to allow for quantum leaps in success. The hands-off manager learns a lot from the negative.

Your decision-making process throughout the day evolves from the process of listening to your wisdom. You may be trying to choose between two options. As you look at one option, how does your body respond to it? Does this option allow you to breathe openly? Does it allow you to have a clear head? Does it allow you to feel a sense of well-being and, ultimately, a sense of accomplishment? Or does it create a feeling of repression, inappropriateness, and negativity?

All you need to succeed is what's already in you. Once you understand that, you can pass it on to the people you manage. It's a revolutionary concept in the workplace. A truly unusual thought. And perhaps this thought goes against every other business book you'll ever read. It certainly contradicts the kind of bleak knowledge that many people describe as "common sense." Actually it is the only sense that is common to all of us.

Transcending the limitations of mind is not possible for dreamers who are addicted to concepts and intellectual abstractions—only to warriors and lovers of truth who are ready to merge with the ecstatic fire of Now.

—Maitreya Ishwara

It's not that this inward warrior's journey is all that easy. It isn't. That's why you are there to mentor it and keep it on track for your people. Because most of your people have spent their whole lives doing everything they do for outside approval, so they're always trying to get immediate external feedback for their every action and decision.

Your work is to help them recover from this toxic addiction to approval. It contaminates their work. Approval-seeking is a sickness that must be cured for them to finally do great work (for which the ultimate approval always comes anyway).

So the true hero's journey is going inside to find your power, because there's no immediate feedback for it. When you're alone, searching your interior, there's no one to say "good job!" as you scan your heart and soul for your true choices. It takes more discipline—not less—than the typical outside-in approach to success.

The hands-off approach carries this key insight: Allowing success is the opposite of forcing success. It is learning what it means to be in alignment with life and with yourself. In due course, you even learn to release yourself from all the "shoulds" that have been placed on you by the world (and your imaginings of the world).

One of the problems people have when they hear something as intriguing as allowing success rather than forcing success, is that they think maybe this is theoretical or spiritual, or something that hasn't ever been used or tried or worked with.

The opposite is true! This is the system that works in the real-world workplace. This is an applied system. It isn't someone imagining what business would be like if it were optimal. This is actually something you can use. If you're a leader sitting across from your people, this is something you can coach them in. It's something you can coach yourself in.

Soon you'll be consistently finding the strengths in your people instead of trying to add what's missing. Soon you'll be able to teach them to use what's inside them, instead of trying to fix them and doing the things most managers try in vain to do.

Most businesses operate through wild attempts at control. They focus on their own rules, policies, detailed supervision, inspections, and quality control, as if their people were trained animals!

The hands-off manager is the solution to that dysfunction. Because when you find people who love to do what you're asking them to do, you don't have to control them. You don't have to motivate them. You don't have to force them to work harder. You don't have to threaten them to get them to perform. They already love doing it so it comes naturally to them.

So what, then, is the manager's job?

Your job as a hands-off manager will be a job of learning. You'll be learning to be aware of what your people love to do. You'll be learning what powers live naturally inside them. You'll then be more skilled at placing people in roles suited to their talents. You will see into them, see what they love to do, and listen to what they tell you. Your best work will be to closely observe what they show you.

It can get interesting and challenging when you embark on this journey, because people don't always tell you the truth! They tell you what they think you want to hear, or what they think will get them a higher salary. That's the curse of approval-seeking in action. You'll detoxify that situation every time you show them that winning your approval is not a productive pursuit; that doing good work will take them further than that every time. When you can mentor people this way you will free them up and they will thank you forever. Approval-seeking is our society's most futile and dysfunctional pursuit. If your people can learn to drop it from their workplace endeavors, they may even learn to drop it at home and improve their personal relationships.

The work, and the love of it, becomes the focus. When you place people in roles for which they are unsuited, you can't supervise them enough or discipline them enough to get good work. Because there's no love there. You can try to impose more policies and procedures, but you still won't get what you're looking for.

But when you place people in roles that are ideally suited for who they are, watch what happens. Now they have a chance to exhibit their gifts and do what they love. So you can walk away and come back later to a job well done with little or no supervision. That's hands-off managing at its best. You weren't even there!

Is this too soft a system? You might worry that it's not tough-minded enough to produce results, but our experience tells us that quite the opposite is true. In fact, this system is exactly what the toughest-minded football coaches do. It's Vince Lombardi walking along a practice field trying to figure out whether his linebacker should really be a safety. Or whether his tight end would be a better fullback. And then finally deciding, "I want to try you out at fullback; the way you move it looks like it's a better fit for you." A focused coach in football will often move players out of the position they think they should be in to something that fits better. The coach sees that as his ongoing role, to match up his athletes, put them in different positions, and keep moving until they're all in positions that come more naturally to them.

In the end, the best coaches and the best leaders are people who will get the best out of their players, as opposed to trying to force something out of them that may not be there. The greatest gift you can give people is to give them themselves. Duane tells his managers, "See more in your people than they're seeing. Then, invite them to your vision."

What loneliness is more lonely than distrust?

—George Eliot

Why do you have to do this? Why do we need mentors to help people do what they love to do? Why can't people already see this potential in themselves?

Because they're trained not to!

In our society's system, most people are beaten down and critical of themselves as they emerge from young adulthood and enter the workplace. Their teenage years have been a blizzard of anxious criticism from worried parents and teachers fearful that their kids would not "turn out," and therefore embarrass them. Then the young people enter the workplace only to get mismanaged by people without any real leadership skills, and their resentment builds. Finally, they are so unable to forgive and forget and move on that they can't see their own abilities anymore. They're already obsessed with how they are being judged and treated by others. So their potential stays hidden under all of the criticism and the "shoulds" they've been living up to all their lives. Is it any wonder that they turn to approval-seeking as their only focus? Rather than focusing on their work, how to fall in love with it and be excellent at it, they are always trying to win approval, score points, make impressions, and criticize others so that they get approval by comparison.

But where is the good work in all of that? We have taught our young people to be aggressive, cynical politicians instead of true craftsmen and masters of their work.

So the real job of our leadership is to give these people back to themselves.

When they are mere approval-seekers they live in fear of criticism. They swing between severe anticipation and imaginary fear. They try to score inner-office impressions instead of pleasing the customer. They think the competition is the person down the hall, not the company making a similar product. And then they wonder why the other company took their customer.

Soon their stress causes them to convert fear of anticipated criticism into self-criticism. Not consciously, but subconsciously the programming may go like this: "I'll criticize myself so that you can't criticize me." Or, "I'll get to me before you can!" Self-criticism and low self-esteem become a defense mechanism. (You will see this in the people you sit down with when you take over a new team. If you're the first hands-off manager they have ever had, it will be like entering a war-torn province.) The worker's subconscious mind says, "If I'm already skeptical of the work I do and who I am in the workplace, then at least I've beaten you to it." It isn't just managers and parents who miss this opportunity to give people to themselves. Sometimes even professional success coaches and consultants miss it—the very people you would think were there to reverse the process. Rather than coaching you into becoming the best of who you are, they look for the best of who they think you should be. That makes the coaching relationship less than supportive, and keeps alive the client's sense of "I can't do this."

Without hands-off management and mentoring that is compassionate and visionary, leadership generally defaults to this philosophy: "The world would be a better place if only everyone would operate as I do." That's an alarmingly narcissistic perspective, and because of that, it's not functional. We are interconnected beings, not isolated egos.

When you blame others, you give up your power to change.

—Douglas Noel Adams

A computer programmer we worked with named Jared was letting his stressful beliefs get in his own way. He was little more than a collection of thoughts about his own weakness. So he lived in fear and set out to make sure his every move won someone's approval. His focus was on his own frightened ego.

There is a mistaken perception in our society that confuses ego with high self-worth. Ego is really the opposite of that. Ego fearfully asserts itself. So, paradoxically, Jared could lose his ego and increase his inner confidence and sense of worth at the same time. Fortunately he had a hands-off manager who saw that.

Jared redirected his focus to the work, realigned with the work he loved most, and soon got so into his work that approval-seeking was no longer necessary. He realized the ultimate: Love what you do and you won't need anyone's approval.

The hands-off football coach

When the University of Texas football team won the national championship in the 2006 Rose Bowl, it was largely due to their star quarterback, Vince Young. Young had become a well-rounded, complete player in his junior year, and many were calling him the best college quarterback of all time. When his coach Mack Brown was asked how all those improvements in Vince Young's game occurred from one year to the next, Coach Brown said, "We just stopped coaching him. We just got out of his way. We saw what was emerging in him, and we decided to let it come forward without a lot of old coaches messing with it."

That was a huge act of both hands-off power and humility on the part of Coach Brown, and he had a national championship to show for it. Most coaches would still be trying to change Vince Young and "correct" him.

Listen to Coach Brown further and you realize that he does not have low self-esteem at all. Quite the contrary: A true and powerful humility is not thinking that you're less than; it's knowing that you're phenomenal. But so is everybody else! So you raise the bar, not only for yourself, but for all those around you when you come from this powerful perspective.

"Sometimes great coaching is knowing what not to do," he said.

Steps to hands-off success in your life

Three action steps to take after reading this chapter:

1. Hold a meeting with your people that is not about the future or the past. Make the meeting be about the here and now: What talents and skills and loves do we now possess? Are we using them well? Center the whole meeting on what's already

great and how we can better use and express it. Just the way a football coach would after a game. Are we all playing the right positions?

2. Look at the next two or three decisions you think you have to make. Sit and write them down. Are you adding stress to these decisions by continuing to think, *I've got to make a decision!* Any stress you add to your day is getting in the way of your team's—and your own—success. So challenge the stressful thought that says you "must" make a decision, and learn to let decisions make themselves. Look at the three decisions you have to make and write notes about the pros and cons of potential choices and notice how your inner vision will make it obvious which choice to make. You didn't have to superimpose the stress of "having to make" a decision on top of this process of allowing the decision to make itself.

3. In your next interview with a candidate who wants to join your team, look at the time you have allotted for the interview and add an hour to it. That extra time will allow you and the candidate to drop all the role-playing that goes on in interviews and simply allow the inner vision to emerge. If the candidate is a good fit, the extra hour will only confirm that for you. If the candidate raises red flags, they will multiply in the next hour and you will know not to make the mistake made by Jack and Melissa earlier in this chapter.

CHAPTER EIGHT
REVERSING YOUR PROCESS

The oak sleeps in the acorn, the bird waits in the egg,
and in the highest vision of the soul a waking angel stirs.
Dreams are the seedlings of realities.

—James Allen

Chuck sat in the conference room fidgeting and nervously asking for coaching about a problem he had with Jodie, the young woman he was teamed with on a customer appreciation project.

"My problem is what Jodie did to me last week," Chuck said. "She hurt me and disappointed me by taking our written proposal to the boss and acting as if it was all hers."

We sat with Chuck for a while as he described his alarming and disappointing outer world and its untrustworthy inhabitants. We then guided him back to the moment. How would you like to feel moving forward? Because, the most wonderful thing about the past is that it's finished and done with forever.

Soon we had invited Jodie into the room with Chuck and we were allowing a new mutual understanding to arise between them by keeping our hands off their conversation and letting them relate to each other in a new way. Jodie had given Chuck a lot of credit in her meeting with the boss, and the two of them began to see that they could support each other in more ways than they'd realized. Chuck's outside world of danger was actually less of a threat than he believed.

After a while the process of mistrust was reversed.

What if all that's going on in the outer world is nothing more than feedback? Opportunities to meet with people and understand them better? Maybe we can, through this reversing process, look at things differently. We can look at situations not for what's wrong, but for what they're telling us about what's possible.

Therefore all of this "opposition," "negative things," and "what we don't want" is merely beneficial feedback in disguise, showing up to help us understand and come to know ourselves. If we fear and judge this feedback, it becomes a barrier to that understanding. It becomes a resistance that blocks the very understanding it's here to reveal.

I am a pilot and I fly a process

Duane Black meets with his people and defuses a stressful situation by saying:

I am a pilot, and therefore, I like the metaphor of flying a plane to explain this process. On a flight, a pilot is always off course. And therefore it's continuous realignment that gets him to his destination. And if there were no such thing as "off course," there could be no flight. Because a flight is a series of realignments from off course to on course. Every step of the way. Even an autopilot operating on a GPS (the technology that keeps you almost perfectly on course) is designed to constantly monitor any minor course deviation and correct that in order to keep you on course. So the way the autopilot functions is also the way a pilot functions, in a constant process of course correction, of altitude correction, of turn and bank correction, until you come into alignment with the correct space. And then as soon as you notice yourself a little bit off course, you make a correction and come into alignment again.

Notice that an autopilot does not get depressed or angry when it's off course. It welcomes that feedback from the environment, because "off course" puts the plane on course.

But a person similar to Chuck will think, merely out of superstition, that there's something wrong with being off course. So he negatively judges that feedback from the environment and gets so upset about it that he can't take in the information it's trying to give him.

A real feeling of being off course for a lot of people on your team will happen whenever there is change. They have a natural resistance to change, and generate a deep inner fear of it. They don't see that change is synonymous with a happy life and a vibrant organization.

It is not the strongest of the species that survives, nor the most intelligent, but the one most responsive to change.

—Charles Darwin

The hands-off manager treats change as the joy and pleasure of living in a four-season environment. You probably enjoy a rainy day once in a while. It nourishes the Earth! The mix, the newness, is what keeps life fresh. Change is what keeps life interesting and what keeps us growing.

The hands-off manager helps her people see that life is a process of becoming and evolving (in other words, changing). And when her people can accept change as a friend, not as an enemy, they've completed another successful reversal.

Look again to the inside

Most managers look outside themselves, at the organization and the world, to see what needs to be fixed. Then they look outside again to see what they want to aspire to. Then they try, through judgment, to change what's in the world to what they think it ought to be.

It's time to reverse this process. Not just at work but in your whole life.

It's time to look at the world only to see your own reflection. The world without is a mirror of what's within. Only by seeing it as a mirror can you learn to alter your internal approach from micromanaging the world to hands-off harmony with its forces.

The first step toward this is to stop thinking so critically. Stop comparing. Stop judging others. Stop trying to determine what people "should" do.

Instead, first discover who they are.

Then discover who you are.

The world outside will act as a mirror reflecting back to you. As you go into it and attempt different things, it will show you what works best for you. Listen to the compliments coming from other people. Listen to what people say about what you're doing. Do they acknowledge how good you are at it? Look to the world almost as a sounding board to give you feedback to help you understand and come to know better what's inside you.

Then see what comes to you naturally. See what you don't have to work so hard to be good at, because that's your gift. Mozart started composing when he was a child. He found it early. And his parents and those around him gave him immediate positive feedback.

There's a gift similar to that in all of us.

So it's time to stop looking externally for what we need to fix out there. Instead, we can look externally for what we align with inside ourselves. And then we can let what we experience communicate to us. Our practice becomes a practice of trusting life. Just as a beginning swimmer learns to trust the water.

Some people we introduce to this practice don't believe that such natural ability is there. Some of them say, "I'm not good at anything. Everything I've ever tried I've failed at." But soon they find out, after careful self-observation, that they have consistently tried to be who others thought they should be, which will almost always end in frustration.

That process must be reversed.

The next thing to learn to reverse is the process of overcoming problems. Most managers believe that overcoming problems is their whole reason for existence. They come to work looking for them and if they don't find them, their superiors soon will. Especially if those superiors are old-school, hands-on micromanagers.

But there's no benefit in trying to solve a problem by focusing exclusively on overcoming it. One must be willing to first look at the bigger picture, the whole system.

The world of micromanagement today has an opposite and dysfunctional approach. Most managers judge their people on noncompliance with the rules, or noncompliance with the dress code, or noncompliance with the amount of vacation time or the amount of work they should have done by the end of the day. It pigeonholes people into a very structured, manipulated, and controlled environment. They do this to get the best out of their employees. But they're getting the worst instead. They are imposing a lockdown mentality in the workplace.

It isn't necessary to imagine the world ending in fire or ice. There are two other possibilities: one is nostalgia, and the other is paperwork.

—Frank Zappa

To truly get the best out of your people, you want to get your hands off their lives. You want to let what's naturally in them come through, not force them into compliance with a predetermined program.

Better communication at work

We enjoy being with people when they're comfortable, natural, and spontaneous. Not when they're trying to be something they're not. We like seeing the real person there.

People who are themselves bring the best out in you. You connect to that relaxed vibration and all of a sudden it helps you be yourself. Because when someone else is putting on airs, you get a little defensive and start to think, "I wonder who I should be?" And then there are two false and competitive egos clashing. But when somebody can relax into the pure being of who they are, it helps you relax into who you are and it creates a great relationship. The workplace settles down. You look forward to coming in.

When you're in alignment, you have come to know who you are in the bigger scheme of things. Your company is no longer an alien object because you have come to know what your company values. You know who your company wants to be in terms of the product it delivers. You know the reputation it has for customer service. So you've already established that principle in yourself. Not a goal to get to, but an inner principle from which to operate. You now have a direction and set of values that define who you are as a person and a company.

From this position it's easy and natural to evaluate work projects skillfully. You endeavor not so much to analyze whether a project is good or bad, but whether it's a fit. You look to see if something is in alignment with what you and your company stand for.

Again, the company Duane works for is about creating midrange to upper-end housing in quality areas. It has become a principle and a place from which to operate.

"We know what we're about," Duane says, "so it is easy and natural for us to look to see what kind of projects might fit into that category. We can make our professional lives about looking to see what we align with. Not what's wrong with things."

That's another reason it's so important to discover and understand who you really are as a team. Because if you don't know that, it's hard to find out what you align with. You don't know what is or is not the best fit for your company's culture.

Creativity is a type of learning process where the teacher and pupil are located in the same individual.

—Arthur Koestler

Just start giving them your time

Many of us in this society grew up learning about the concept of tithing, the idea that if I give 10 percent of my income to good causes I will actually have more. But you can't make that work on an adding machine! You can't make that work out analytically.

Yet our experience has been that when we are generous and giving, we do somehow seem to end up with more instead of less. That's a true principle of life. But it will not work analytically. It will only work as an inner awareness. But most people go through life on guard. They go through life with a need to protect themselves. They try to limit their risks and watch out for who's trying to hurt them. That's their barrier to this hands-off process of discovery. They don't know how to let the world communicate with them to show them what's inside themselves, because they're too busy protecting themselves from the world.

This is even more true in companies. I was recently coaching employees at a Fortune 500 superstar company, and most of the people I spoke to thought the company itself was the enemy. They started their sentences out with "This company doesn't…" or "This company never…."

One of the ways you know your hands-off management is succeeding is when you hear your people say, "Our company is..." or "We always...." It's an inclusive "our" and "we" versus an exclusive, antagonistic "they" or "them."

It's no wonder companies descend into this paranoid, self-protecting culture. Our whole society feels absolutely trapped in this syndrome. Try to sell a newspaper about good news! Try to start a television news station based on the positive things happening in the world. As the old saying in the newspaper business goes, "If it bleeds, it leads." People have conditioned themselves not to look for what's possible, but for what's dangerous. When we vote for our presidents, one of the biggest selling points seems to be which one is going to protect us the most; not who can lead us into the kind of future we want to have, but who can protect us from evil?

To have happiness and success on our work team we must reverse this process ourselves. We can't wait for society and the rest of the world to wake up. And we start by looking at our people as great people. And then looking for what's possible instead of what's wrong.

The magic formula that successful businesses have discovered is to treat customers like guests and employees like people.

—Tom Peters

Begin to watch every thought—it might be an opportunity for a turnaround in your belief system. Get good at that kind of reversal. Is that thought life-enhancing? Is it a thought that communicates to you and your team an example of who you are and who you wish to become? Or is it this thought: *I wonder if that person wants to hurt* me? Or, *I wonder if this person just wants my job, or if they're just telling me that to get on my good side?*

Our biggest opportunity as managers is to reverse all we've been taught and start to think in terms of what could be, instead of what should be but isn't.

It's not natural to want to hide and live in fear and desperation. It's normal and common, but it's not natural. And the reason we know it's not natural is that we've never met anyone who felt a sense of peace who lived in that way.

Physically we're more advanced in this awareness than we are mentally or spiritually. Physically, when we experience pain, we immediately realize that something is out of alignment. So we work to bring it back into alignment through whatever means we can: nutrition, physical therapy, even surgery. We want to get ourselves back into the flow of things. Spiritually and mentally, though, when there's pain, we blame others! We think, superstitiously, there's something outside of us that needs fixing. So try to fix the world outside.

But the world outside is only a reflection of the pain inside. So we're chasing ourselves. Want to be miserable? Try chasing yourself.

The hands-off manager calls off the chase.

Steps to hands-off success in your life

Three action steps to take after reading this chapter:

1. Write down three things you wish hadn't happened at work last week.

2. Under each incident put the words, "Course Correction," and list the ways you can make things better because of this so-called negative event. What can you use the event for? How can it be a parable or teaching tool in the future? What was it sent here to show you?

3. Before you announce a change to your team or to an individual, do a little brainstorming with yourself. All change is growth toward the better. The universe is kind. What is stopping you from seeing and communicating this? What homework can you do on this change so you can sell it enthusiastically to your team instead of sharing in their grief about it?

CHAPTER NINE
TUNING YOUR INSTRUMENT

Harmony is not just a feeling. It's a physical process.

—Dr. Rollin McCraty

There is help for us in discovering what we align with.

There are books written about muscle testing and how you actually have a physical response to thoughts. Your body gets weaker or stronger based on how a certain thought is affecting you. (We recommend *Power Versus Force* by David Hawkins.)

Duane uses a breathing process in which he tries to figure out whether something is constraining his ability to breathe freely and easily, or whether he feels open around it. Some people call it gut instinct, but whatever process you use, you want to become aware of yourself physically.

As I've said, we understand alignment when it comes to physical pain. We understand indigestion. We understand fatigue. We know how to read those signals. But it is less natural for us to stop to read the more subtle implications of misalignment, especially misalignment in our lives and our minds. We get so busy that we don't take a moment to feel how things are affecting us. Do I feel disappointed or sad by this circumstance? Do I feel a sense of well-being and peace? Do I feel joy around this person, or do I feel discomfort and anxiety around him?

Almost everyone knows when they're in the presence of someone with whom they feel comfortable. There's a feeling. It's not even rational—it's not because that person uses big words or dresses a certain way. That may have attracted you to (or repelled you from) him initially, but as you get to know him, your comfort level comes from an inner connection you feel. An emotional connection.

There can be no knowledge without emotion. We may be aware of a truth, yet until we have felt its force, it is not ours. To the cognition of the brain must be added the experience of the soul.

—Arnold Bennett

If you're going to allow success in your life, if you're going to create a life of peace and joy and satisfaction, you've got to become aware of and sensitive to what you align with. And you've got to discipline yourself to go there, to know what fits you best, to eat the kind of foods that contribute to your health, to engage in exercise that contributes to your physical well-being, to breathe air that is beneficial. It's how alignment breeds success and well-being.

What we're most ignorant of is how this alignment originates in our thinking. What thoughts bring us a sense of well-being? What thoughts bring us a sense of comfort, joy, and peace? If you are willing to notice it you can begin by deliberately nurturing those aligned thoughts.

You can also dismantle and dissolve thoughts that lead you away from success. Those are the thoughts that make you angry, sad, afraid, and disappointed; any thoughts that incite the fear-based emotions. Shine your light on them. Look at how they are positive course-corrections in disguise. Do not be afraid of them. Do not take them literally or seriously. If they are negative, they are not in alignment with the universe.

You may need to consider choosing a different position in the company if you find that as hard as you're trying, the work you're doing just isn't fulfilling. But if you're *afraid of change*, what can you do? Stay paralyzed and miserable? When you believe your negative thoughts, any possibility for bold change looks too difficult. That's where the previous chapter on reversal becomes vital and useful. Because once you've altered your approach to life so that you can reverse whatever thoughts you wish, you will actually look forward to change. You will look forward to many of the very things you used to fear.

Once you have reversed your feelings about change, you can change anything, including your job. You can use the feedback mechanism inherent in this altered process to look from the inside out instead of the outside in and discover where you belong. You'll feel what works best for you.

When we practice this we are focused on where we want to go, not what we want to get away from. So we can focus our whole lives on alignment. And when something doesn't fit, it's not bad or wrong—it's a form of beneficial communication! Misalignment is a teacher who tells you, "This doesn't fit with you. This isn't an alignment with who you naturally are. You won't find success here. With this line of thinking, you'll only find obstacles."

We've heard so much, and so many books have been written about your life's purpose. Some people say their life's purpose is to be a teacher, or an artist, or a CEO, or a spiritual leader. And yes, those purposes can apply, but what we are talking about is *bigger than that*.

Your purpose is to become who you are

All those professions and callings may be eventual aspects of your purpose. Wonderful manifestations of it. But your highest purpose is to become the fulfillment of your potential. Right now, in this eternal moment. Not in some distant, hard-won future.

Your purpose is to learn to manifest and bring into the world the gifts that are contained within you. Now. It is simply the most fundamental, the most profound, and the most important reason for living. It's to become who you already are. That's your purpose. That's everyone's purpose.

What if—just for a moment—you could live without any thoughts of money? What if you could live beyond all thoughts of need? What if you only showed up at work today to do what you most love to do? How would that be? Who would you be? That's a good exercise to begin with.

And then we might go even further than that. Discovering our purpose is about *gaining an understanding of it*. It happens in silence and solitude. It's not uncovered by reading 35 books on how to discover your life's purpose.

Purpose is simple. Purpose is letting the best of what's in you come through and then giving it to the world. That's your life's purpose. And everyone has the same purpose! No exceptions. And within that purpose, they have their individual outer manifestation of it: their gift to entertain, their gift to organize, their gift to teach, their gift to create.

The best way of leading people is to let them find their own way.

—Byron Katie

When Robert DeNiro acted in *Raging Bull* he channeled the boxer Jake LaMotta. He "became" that person. He studied him, he gained weight to look like him, and he so became him that it was as though he were LaMotta. If DeNiro can do it with a dead boxer, you can do it with yourself.

I remember being at a standstill in the mid 1980s. I was at a crossroads in my life and I had no idea what to do next in my career. And I just thought, *When was I happiest?* I thought back to a 12-step meeting I was in when I was talking to a large room full of people. And I thought, *I've never been happier, less aware of time passing, more connected to the human race than at that moment.* And that's when I made my decision: *Okay, I'm going to be a speaker. I'm doing seminars and giving talks. That's it.*

When I told Duane about this he said to me, "The reason your seminars have been so successful is you are yourself! Not who you think you ought to be. You don't have to create some story about having been a war hero. The audience connects to you because you've had problems and you've figured out a way to let them go and you have no shame in telling about them. And that's where a lot of your audience is. They connect to you and they align with that life of problems. If you told them you were a war hero and never made a mistake in your life, they would not align with you."

Alignment is the key to channeling your higher self. Being yourself, you come into alignment. You understand what that means. Now you're doing it. Now you're listening to your emotions, listening to your feelings, listening to your body, listening to your breath, and listening to your fatigue.

When you do something you absolutely love, you can do it for hours without even getting tired. When you do something you can hardly stand, in a matter of minutes you're exhausted, so you can see why aligning with what you love brings the energy and focus that spells success. Once you see this in yourself, you'll see it in your people; once this principle kicks in for you, it will be your biggest gift to them.

You might be thinking, *How do I know what I'm good at?* All you have to do is listen and learn. Listen to the environment and other people. Pay attention, because they're trying to tell you what you're good at all the time! It's in you, but there's also feedback—the world is trying to tell you who you are. There are signals. It's all a big mirror of your own soul. If you feel wonderful when you read a sentence in a book and somehow you get goose bumps, that's the world trying to say, "That's you!"

Steps to hands-off success in your life

Three action steps to take after reading this chapter:

1. Take a few breaks today to just be with yourself and listen to your inner voice. It can be for 30 seconds with your eyes closed and your breathing deep. Watch what happens when you do this.

2. Start thinking in terms of alignment and misalignment rather than right and wrong. Notice that "right" and "wrong" are violent judgments compared to the gentle nature of alignment and misalignment.

3. Use your negative feelings as a welcome alarm clock. Let them lead you back to the stressful thought in question. Use that thought to make the workplace better.

CHAPTER TEN
BECOMING AVAILABLE

Intuition is the clear conception of the whole at once.

—Johann Kaspar Lavater

If we are the old-school micromanagers, we've been in hiding. We've been unavailable. We have disguised who we are.

We've been hiding behind a disguise made up of our problems and the excuses for having those problems. We've been cloaked in a robe of alibis, hiding behind a disguise that says we consist of our unsolved problems, that who we are is a composition of our unsolved problems in life!

We've taken on this identity instead of our true potential, and because we've done that, we've made ourselves unavailable to the very freedom for which we yearn.

So it's time to turn and go another way, to calmly choose another path to take. This path will make you available to yourself. It will make you available to the inherent wisdom contained in who you already are.

Old-school micromanagers try hard to learn how to succeed. They seek out teachers and success gurus. They want to think and grow rich. But it's that very thinking that's in the way.

They don't realize that a better approach would be to *stop thinking* and grow rich.

Even Galileo knew that the answer was not in outside knowledge. He said, "You cannot teach a person anything. You can only help him discover it within himself."

Galileo's words are the heart and soul of hands-off management.

Let's say you've cleared your mind and learned to disarm all the negative thoughts in your life as they arise. Now you're free to discover who you are. You're free to realize the best that's in you. Soon you begin to see what you can really accomplish and bring into the world.

What's really happened? *You have become available to yourself.* And in this freedom from all those burdens and baggage you've been carrying, you're able to follow your instincts. Because you listen to your instincts now. You're not worried about what Susie three cubicles down might have said about you today. You're available for inner ideas. You're available for insights. Your mind is quiet and open to new ideas. You're available for inspiration.

It will feel like you've taken down the Great Wall of China. You've erased that wall you have built in yourself through a lifetime of criticism, self-judgment, anger, and disappointment—all the thoughts that have blocked your potential from coming through. You no longer grab and hang on to thoughts that say to you, *Life isn't fair, Gee, I'm a victim, I'm not responsible,* or *This shouldn't have happened to me.*

Now you let those thoughts pass. You give them no life or credibility. You laugh at them now because you know they're not true.

In fact, you attach your beliefs to none of your thoughts; you just continue to learn to go deeper than thought, and listen.

The only real valuable thing is intuition.

—Albert Einstein

Perhaps you've heard the admonition "You can't listen while you're talking." That's even more true for your inner dialogue. So you learn to reverse your patterns so that your mental process is much less about thinking and much more about listening. Soon you grow quieter. You don't need to share all your ideas with everybody, because you're no longer trying to fix everybody. You've moved on from that. You've accepted them for who they are, and you're accepting without judgment their weaknesses and their problems. In fact, you don't even label them "problems" anymore. They're just energy patterns in life as fascinating as anything else.

People don't have any power over you anymore because a deeper you is in control now. Not the shallow, scared ego.

Now you're available to receive intuitive insights from deep inside yourself. You're not going over and over in your head how you wish you would have responded to that criticism. You don't prepare your defense every time you get a difficult e-mail from your supervisor.

You're not overloading your mental bandwidth with how you wish you had come back with some coarse remark that would have made someone feel as bad as they "made" you feel. You understand that's a waste of time. They can't "make" you feel anything. Only your thoughts can do that. You laugh at the idea of indulging those kind of thoughts now.

You're only interested in realizing your potential— becoming who you already are! You realize that your potential lies within you; it is not out there in the future. You don't have to *get anywhere* to have realized your potential. Your potential is yours to feel inside you, right here and right now. Beating like a heart.

When you're living the hands-off life, the outside world will begin responding to you differently because you'll be more open to opportunity. You might be in that quiet place where a person just pops into your mind, and you will go to your computer and send that person a nice note. The next thing you know, that person is calling and saying, "I have some business for you. I've been meaning to talk to you."

That's *allowing success* instead of trying to force it to happen.

Steps to hands-off success in your life

Three action steps to take after reading this chapter:

1. Take out a notebook and write down a negative thought you had today about someone at work. Challenge the thought as if you were that person's defense attorney. Is it really true? Is the negative feeling you get when you think that thought really worth it?

2. Give that person a call and talk for a few minutes in an open and warm way, finding out what life is like for him right now. (If you can do this in person, all the better. Drop by his workstation just to ask how he's doing and how you can help.)

3. After you've met with him, go back to the negative thought you initially wrote down and see if it has any truth or power left. Notice that negative thoughts isolate you from people, while positive thoughts connect you with them.

CHAPTER ELEVEN
LETTING GO OF JUDGMENT

If you judge people, you have no time to love them.

—Mother Teresa

Doug was a top-level salesperson who had just lost a huge deal. He was selling corporate training programs and the company he was selling to was suddenly being purchased by another company. Fortunately for Doug, his manager, Tony, who was a friend of ours, was also a hands-off master mentor.

Tony listened to Doug's story about what had happened for a while but refused to mirror Doug's long face and sad voice. When Doug expressed his final frustration about losing the big contract, hands-off Tony just winked at him.

"You're great," said Tony, "and this is not bad news."

"Not bad news? We had a $700,000 contract disappear and it's not bad news?"

"It's just what happened."

"Well, I'm tired of this Zen stuff or whatever it is. I was counting on that commission."

Tony said, "Let's work with what is. Let's look at all news as good news. At least potentially."

Doug said, "But how can I close a deal with them if they are in negotiation to sell the company? The company won't even be theirs. They can't sign the check!"

"How is this good news?" asked Tony.

"It's not," said Doug after thinking for a while.

"What if the training you are offering them could help them get a better price for their company? What if the fact that they'd contracted for transformative training and begun to implement it increased the perceived value of the company?"

Doug said nothing, but his demeanor suggested that he was getting interested.

His manager, Tony, continued, "They've done our pilot training trial courses for two months now and the employees got a real boost, so they want to roll out the big program, right?"

"Until the sale of the company, yes."

"Right! So now they can go into negotiations having invested in a powerful training boost to productivity. It allows the buyer to perceive this company as thirsty for ongoing improvement. It also allows the seller to suggest that the bottom-line numbers are about to get much better because of what this training can produce. They can increase their price in the sale of the company. Everybody wins."

Doug was lit up. He thanked Tony and left the room ready to make the pitch of his life. The end of this story was a happy one for Doug, because the client bought the training as a bargaining chip in the sale negotiation, and ended up not selling after all. The employee base was so rejuvenated by the training that the original owners decided to keep the company and grow it.

Had Doug's hands-off manager Tony not shown Doug how to drop the negative judgment and just work with what happened, gloom and doom would have been in Doug's life for weeks after the "bad news" arrived.

Tony was unusual. Hands-off managers are one in a million. Most employees are led by ineffective micromanagers who suffer from their own habit of continuous judgment.

The common theme of most managers is that they are always at least mildly upset about what's happening. You see it in their faces, hear it in their voices, read it in their e-mails.

But what's happening is not upsetting them. Their judgment about it is.

Anything that bothers us only bothers us because we have a judgment about it. We cling to passing thoughts that say, *This is wrong! This shouldn't be happening to me!* But we don't stop to realize that the upset we're experiencing is caused by our judgment.

If we could be open to all things and see them as the *flow of the marketplace* and get away from *what should not be*, we would release ourselves from a monumental amount of dissatisfaction, upset, stress, and blame.

This ability to dismiss judgment when it pops up is a critical skill for the hands-off manager to cultivate. It takes daily practice, but the practice is rewarding beyond measure.

In my experience, the best creative work is
never done when one is unhappy.

—Albert Einstein

If you drop this negative judgment long enough, it will produce peace at your center and a gentle surge of relaxed intelligence that can deal well with any issue.

We aren't saying you should be in denial. We aren't recommending that you not evaluate. You can evaluate without passing personal judgment. You can be an expert evaluator of performance, without being disappointed in or upset about a person's actions.

Knowing the difference is vital.

A coworker in a top managerial position was recently going through a lot of stress about a circumstance her son was in. She thought her state was caused by her son and his circumstances, but it wasn't. There was only one thing that was really a problem for her: her judgment. But she couldn't see it. She was looking at his illness, his financial struggles, and his marital struggles as things that *should not be happening*. It was reality, but to her, reality was wrong.

And that *belief* was the cause of her stress. Not her son. Her son had nothing to do with it. Her thoughts were the only "bad thing" that was "happening to" her, but she was old-school judgmental and could not see it.

Her stress was fundamentally triggered by her belief that what she was going through *shouldn't be happening*. She had placed herself firmly in non-acceptance, resistance, and judgment. And that self-placement was creating her suffering.

The beauty of seeing all this is that it allows you to release yourself from stress. When stress leaves you, your physical well-being improves dramatically. You don't need as much rest. You're naturally more optimistic and hopeful. You look forward to the day!

Your direct reports will be grateful. Wouldn't you be if you were them? If you were an employee, what kind of manager would you want? One who looked forward to her day? Or one who was always stressed?

We recall a recent coaching session with a young IT worker starting with this question, "How stressed does your manager get?"

"It's off the charts."

"And what does he do with this stress?"

"He takes it out on us."

How much relaxed and happy productivity will emerge from that employee?

Everything that irritates us about others can lead us to an understanding of ourselves.

—Carl Gustav Jung

As a hands-off manager you can be different. You can start your day centered in the peaceful, present-moment awareness of infinite possibility. And that's because you no longer imagine all the things that are going to go wrong. There is no "wrong" way in which things can go. They're just going to go where they're going to go. There's no more judgment about what's going to occur. This allows you to be much more in the moment.

Notice that all the challenges you've faced that you judged negatively at the time ended up contributing to your strength and growth. The "bad breaks" all eventually contributed to your understanding. When you get enough time and distance to see the big picture, you almost always see this.

"When I was getting divorced I thought it was the worst thing that ever happened to me," a company engineering manager named Brent said. "But looking back...it was the best thing. The very best thing."

All these "bad things" that happen at work have helped us mature and become more understanding of how to run this business well. And it's "bad things" that can open up this eventual spirit of acceptance. So how "bad" were they? Did we really need to judge them at all?

We are not saying to take a passive attitude. This is the opposite of passive. It's an active embrace of what is. It frees up energy that had previously been trapped in internal conflict and distress. You are ready to act sooner. This is the path of action. It's only passive when you imagine it. It's active when you use it.

Manage agreements, not expectations

You've seen the energy toll taken on stressed-out managers. They are trying to manage their own chaotic universe. They are constantly being pulled back and forth between expectations and disappointments. How much energy is left over to create agreements? How much energy is left to innovate? How much energy is left to bring people together and forge new understandings? Practically zero. Stress has taken the energy away.

Non-judgment opens you up to respond to situations in creative ways. You don't have to settle for anything mediocre. You can change all the things you want. Only now you can change them in a spirit of cooperation instead of a spirit of opposition to the way things are.

Just for today, don't try to fix the world outside. Get busy evolving the world inside. You're working on the joy and freedom that arise when you practice releasing yourself from judgment.

Judgment will always come to your mind now and then, but now you just let it pass through without clinging to it or believing the judgment to be the truth. It's not the truth. It's just a passing stressful thought. As the clouds pass, so can your thoughts.

Life is not so much about what's going on but how we're choosing to interpret it. When someone greets you with, "What's happening?" a more accurate greeting might have been, "How are you judging what's happening?"

It's the ultimate in self-terrorizing stress to believe a passing thought that says something "shouldn't have happened." When in fact it happened! Was it God's first mistake? Was it the universe making a wrong turn? Or was it just as it was supposed to have happened for your benefit and learning?

Soon you alter all your thinking to be about you and your interpretations, instead of the "bad" and "wrong" and "unfair" things that have happened. Soon you realize that your job is not to fix the external world, but rather to beautify the internal world of spirit and mind interacting all day. As the song says, "Let there be peace on earth, and let it begin with me."

Huge, practical benefits arise from this managerial approach. Your people will be eminently more comfortable with you when you accept them the way they are. They will be so much more trusting of you. Now their interest will turn to doing great work for you, whereas before they were playing victim to win your sympathy. Your people want to tell you the truth, particularly when they don't fear being reprimanded for telling you something you don't want to hear.

Once they find out you aren't judging them, they'll share almost anything with you. They are open to creating new agreements.

That's when you can make real progress in helping them improve their skills. The hands-off manager has the rare ability to enter into a true partnership devoted to the success of the employee. Employees who aren't being judged are far more open to coaching and mentoring, and allowing their managers to help them improve.

> You can't depend on your judgment when
> your imagination is out of focus.
>
> —Mark Twain

Think of your best friend right now. When you have a close friend, the first thing that gets suspended is judgment. If you've done something you're not proud of or gotten yourself in a real pickle, your friend is very welcoming and says, "Come talk to me about it. What have you done now?" And he has a big smile on his face because he really doesn't judge you. The friendship is a great friendship because of its lack of judgment.

Non-judgment opens up the door for everyone to be your friend. For everyone to trust you. They can sense in being with you that you don't react negatively to what they say because you're not judging it, even though they're talking to you about something that is completely foreign to anything you would personally do. Maybe they're talking to you about having had a major drug addiction, and you've never even tried drugs. But you're not nursing and clinging to a judgment about that. You're listening.

People who accept us completely are the best friends we have. They will take us in no matter what we do and say, "Hey, don't worry about it. I'm your friend. I'm here to help you. Tell me what I can do."

Steps to hands-off success in your life

Three action steps to take after reading this chapter:

1. The next time someone in a meeting brings up a situation generally accepted to be "bad news" or a negative turn of events, stop the proceedings and slow the meeting down by putting the topic up on the white board.
2. Now invite everyone in the room to participate in an exercise called "What's Good About This?"
3. Go around the room and let people open their imaginations to possible positive outcomes that you didn't immediately see. Do this often enough and you will be training your people in letting go of negative judgment and getting right into positive, creative action, no matter what happens.

CHAPTER TWELVE
CREATING RESULTS

There is peace in the garden. Peace and results.

—Ruth Stout

"We've got to get this thing churning cash flow today!" said Judith, the name we'll use for a team leader I was coaching. "We can't wait until tomorrow!"

"Why can't you do the kinds of things in your workplace that will build a better company in time?" I asked.

"My job is to do it now," she snapped. "I have investors. I have people watching me. And now I have angry customers to deal with."

"Why can't you partner with those customers and give them what they want?"

133

"They want refunds!"

"Why not give them?"

"We can't help customers by giving them a refund on something they really don't deserve a refund on, because that will affect my profits this week."

So I pointed out to Judith that companies such as Nordstrom have built an almost unparalleled success curve in the retail industry by being in it for the long run. They want to build a reputation. They sell quality products and stand by them. And if anyone brings them back, they will give them a refund. No questions asked.

Nordstrom succeeded by focusing on their internal process rather than immediate outcomes. They knew that if they got it right internally, success would come. The paradox is that the more one cares for the internal, the better the external result will be. Results are created by looking inside, whether it's inside a company or inside a human being.

To be successful in business, I want to produce a good product or service. I also want to create a commitment inside my organization to provide a high level of customer service and customer delight. And to achieve these outer results, I now know to look inside the organization. To study the inner system first.

If I also want to have a good sales and marketing program, I'll need good people in my organization to execute our plan. And I now know that if I do that, the results will show up naturally. Enough tuning on the inside and we can just allow external success to occur.

By now these might seem like obvious approaches, but most companies don't do things this way (which may be why four out of five companies fail before reaching their fifth year).

Duane Black has seen company after company in the home-building business focus only on their percentage of profit in every final sale. That's all they think about all day long because that's why they think they're in business. That's how they think they'll be successful. External profit. They focus daily on the final, outside result. As Duane says:

And every one of them I observed closely had their profit margins decline over the years, because all they focused on was the bottom line. Over time they would find themselves in an ever more competitive environment delivering an average level of product, an average level of customer service, and an average level of community. But customers don't want to pay a premium for "average." Customers don't get excited about "average." And so these companies ended up not making big margins. Soon they had to do bigger volume to try to offset their mediocre product. And their volume negatively affected their quality, so the spiral went downward and it wasn't long before they were in real trouble. That's the tragedy of a purely outside focus.

Duane's many years in the highly successful SunCor Development Company have been characterized by the company's inside focus. He's helped lead their commitment to working on the inside rather than the outside.

SunCor decided long ago not to obsess about volume of sales. It trusts that volume will occur naturally; it allows volume to show up when volume is appropriate. It's more focused each day on perfecting the inner system that will create great communities and phenomenal land planning. For example, it insists on always having good architecture, it builds only in great locations, and it boasts a staff of people who love what they do and are aligned with it, and therefore are naturally, effortlessly committed to doing a great job.

The company has also thrived on a noncompetitive, nonintimidating sales environment. Allowing success to occur naturally rather than trying to force it. As Duane says:

We don't say to our salespeople "You will sell 10 houses every month." If we have a month of really bad weather and no one comes to our sales center and they don't sell any houses that month, we don't have a problem with that. We have said to them, "Look at the opportunity you have, here. You get to represent a quality community. You get to represent a quality home. You get to represent people who you know are going to follow through and deliver the product you're promising. What an opportunity you have to be successful. You don't even have to work hard at this. You just get to share with people the incredible opportunity that being in this community would be for them."

Salespeople know they're telling the truth when they sell this way. And customers know the company will take care of them after they buy. They know from SunCor's history that their house will grow in value over time. So it's not a hard sale. If you're a SunCor salesperson you don't have to decide whether your chair should be higher than the customer's during negotiation, or when you should push back from the desk, or when you should be silent because this is a "closing moment." All of those artificial and manipulative strategies don't have to play a role in the process.

All you have to do to be successful as a salesperson is to share what you're excited about and proud of. Share what's inside you. Customers respond to that and it becomes an easy sale. Salespeople succeed when they know what they're really selling. When they know that final, intangible experience of joy that a homeowner feels from moving into just the right home.

Business guru Tom Peters gives seminars on the importance of inner design versus outer striving. On one of his slides he quotes a Harley-Davidson executive who said, "What we sell is the ability for a 43-year-old accountant to dress in black leather, ride through small towns, and have people be afraid of him." The hands-off manager helps a salesperson go inside to find out what they are really selling.

Going inside is used by Duane when he negotiates with landowners to do joint ventures with SunCor. That's why he's been able to make buys that make people around him say, "I can't believe you did that. Why would anybody do a deal like that? How could you buy 20,000 acres for $100,000 down and no payments except out of sales?"

Because the landowner became a partner. The landowner was excited to be a part of what SunCor was doing. He wanted to share in the same passion for producing something to be proud of. It wasn't because his accountant told him it was the best short-term deal he could get. It wasn't because it was the highest amount of up-front value or the most immediately profitable. It was because he felt in his heart that it was how he would be most successful over the long run. He knew that partnering in a sincere quest for quality would likely bring him the most value over time.

This dramatizes the contrast between quick-hit, immediate results–oriented goals (the hands-*on* approach), and long-term purpose and inner intentions (the hands-*off* approach). Duane says:

> *I don't like goals that are results-oriented at all. We don't use them in our organization. Sure, we have forecasts to help our financial planning, but we don't have goals. Therefore we don't think,* Man, am I disappointed in myself because I didn't sell 10 this month. *Our inner dialogue is,* I only sold nine this month, and that's

okay, because look at the way I pleased these people. And look at the way I took care of my customers. And look at the quality of what we delivered. And you know what, they'll tell other people. And next month, I'll probably sell 11! So I'm not worried about it. I show up happy and optimistic every day because I am proud of what we do and who we are.

Duane doesn't want his people to have such an attachment to results that not getting them will make them feel discouraged:

We don't want to feel unhappy with ourselves or unsuccessful because we didn't accomplish numerically what we said we were going to do, because we did accomplish what we said we were going to do. We delivered a good product. We represented it openly and honestly. We took care of these people after the sale. We provided great service and warranty. We did all those things. Those were our goals. Those were the standards we set for ourselves. They were based in who we were going to be, and the doing just naturally took care of itself.

Trust the universe to reward the inside game. It's a process of being who you want to be right now, this very moment, instead of straining to reach a future goal.

Duane recalls a development project in southern Utah, a home-building environment where new community developers don't have a great track record and so are not generally trusted in the beginning. Therefore, when SunCor started a community there, they were working hard to get any sale they could get.

In the first year they sold fewer than 50 homes. The second year it went up to 80. The third year it was up to 100. And the fourth year was just under 120.

"And then, all of a sudden, people realized that we were what we said we were," Duane says. "The community we were building was not just talking about something that was going to turn out great—it *was* turning out great. And the people who lived there were telling their friends, 'This isn't something where they just say they take care of you after the sale; we've been taken care of after the sale.'"

Now they've jumped from 120 houses to more than 200 a year.

"We can't keep up with it!" says Duane. "We're having to limit our sales because we cannot deliver as much product as people want to buy from us. We can't develop the lots fast enough, we can't find enough help to build all the houses we can sell."

The key here was an absence of stressful external goals. They never focused on how many houses they were going to sell to accomplish this level of success—they had the ingredients of success built in. It was an inner process they committed to, followed through on, and delivered.

"So the inner workings were our true goals," says Duane. "They were process goals rather than outcome goals. Our enduring desire was to build a quality product. To provide good customer service. And the other goals—the goals of result, the goals of success—we didn't have them; we didn't need them. We let things flow naturally from the inner commitment to who we were going to be. The desire to be great and the belief that the inner process will create that."

Desire is the starting point of all achievement, not a hope, not a wish, but a keen pulsating desire which transcends everything.

—Napoleon Hill

In *Good to Great*, Jim Collins contrasts companies that have been consistently great over long periods of time with companies that have had their ups and downs. What he found is that over the long haul, the great companies outperform the companies that have the ups and downs by multiples. He didn't even look at companies that hadn't been in business for 50 years or more. The fundamental difference between the two is that the companies that have the ups and downs are the companies that are committed to results only. And the companies that consistently grow and outperform over time are the companies that are committed to being great companies. To taking care of their customers, offering great products, and providing great service. Over the long haul it pays off in multiples. These companies have perfected the inner process, and the outer takes care of itself.

This concept applies to our personal lives, as well. We don't need a goal for how big a house we're going to have. We don't need a goal for how much money we're going to make. If we really want those things, then what we really need is a goal for how good a job we're going to do right now in this hour we are living in.

We can allow the results to emerge in the world outside of us if we take care of our world inside. And there's so much less stress. You never need to be disappointed when you have a "down month" in results. Down months happen. There's nothing wrong with them. But if your quality of work keeps evolving upward, better and better results over the long run will show up. They have to. The universe cannot resist that. It can't help but reward that.

A friend of ours who was a banker said once that banks should not resist high interest rates and economic downturns, because it provides a chance for them to retrench and retrain their people, build new branches, and grow their human capital— in other words, to flow with reality rather than oppose it. Then, when the market turns, they are positioned to take full advantage of the opportunity.

Imagine a life in which you breathe out but you never breathe in. Imagine a life in which you're awake all the time, and you never sleep or stop to rest. Such a life, both physically and mentally, could never work. You have to have your ins and outs and ups and downs. They are part of the dance of life. Down time and up time are both good.

There will be times when you go all out to keep up with the activity. And then there are slower times. One time supports the other. It's the rhythm of life. But people want to make the down time bad and the up time good. That's what throws them off their rhythm and creates professional stress and failure. Rather than resting during down time, they stress out, and a stressed out person does not perform well.

Everyone knows that you are more productive during the day if you get your rest during the night. Everyone knows that if you get a certain level of exercise and a certain level of nutrition, you have the ability to perform at a higher level, because you feel better.

That's all we're talking about here. Allowing success is merely learning to be the kind of person who feels better! Get your rest. Focus on inner things that produce results, then let the results show up naturally. Take away the expectation of outcome and just let things show up. Your every act of relaxed kindness to others will connect down the line.

Throughout this process it helps to allow yourself to see and realize the inner connectedness of all things. To see how one thing relates to everything else. As Duane says:

> *When you sell a home, it affects not only the person buying it, but also their family, the people who come to visit them, and the subsequent owners of that home. It affects the people who work for you who get to build it, the subcontractors, the people who work for them, the city that provides the plan reviews and the inspection process, and the utility companies that deliver the*

electricity, telephone, and cable TV. So many people are affected by that one, simple transaction. It's amazing.

In this success process as it applies to an organization, it's very helpful to eliminate all forms of internal competition. You're not in an organization to do better than the guy two doors down from you; you're in an organization to *work with* the person two doors down from you.

Duane had someone ask him once, "You've been pretty successful inside of a corporate environment; I wouldn't have expected that, because you were self-employed for 17 years before you went there. How did you do it?"

"You know, it was amazingly easy," Duane replied. "I thought of other companies in our industry as my competition, not other people in my organization as my competition. I just chose to focus on how I could do a better job, not on who was getting more attention than I was."

Most people compete internally. They focus on who's getting more recognition from their boss than they are. They obsess about who got a raise that they didn't. They want to point out who took more vacation time than they did. Who left for lunch early.

Whereas to really succeed all they would have had to focus on was: *What can I do to help us be a better company?* They would then be the ones getting all the raises and all the promotions.

All you need to focus on to get ahead is: *What can I give?* Recognize that this isn't a competition, it's a cooperation. You get further ahead by working *with* people. You honor your imagination and theirs. That's how you create results—in this new global society more than ever before!

"The sun is setting on the Information Society," writes Rolf Jensen in *The Dream Society: How the Coming Shift from Information to Imagination Will Transform Your Business*:

> *...even before we have fully adjusted to its demands as individuals and as companies. We have lived as hunters and as farmers, we have worked in factories and*

now we live in an information-based society whose icon is the computer. We stand facing the fifth kind of society: the Dream Society.... Future products will have to appeal to our hearts, not to our heads. Now is the time to add emotional value to products and services.

The hands-off manager is the appropriate person to lead people through the coming shift from information to imagination.

Steps to hands-off success in your life

Three action steps to take after reading this chapter:

1. Rather than listing external goals you want to achieve, start listing inner qualities you want to cultivate and grow. What makes a great leader? List those qualities and score yourself on each so you can track inner progress.

2. Study the interior workings of your team so that you can meet with people about inner strengths instead of outer objectives. Have a meeting to discuss the internal tune-ups needed, and allow people to brainstorm fearlessly.

3. Create a survey for everyone you work with (including yourself) that allows them to identify internal improvements that can be made. Reward the best ideas.

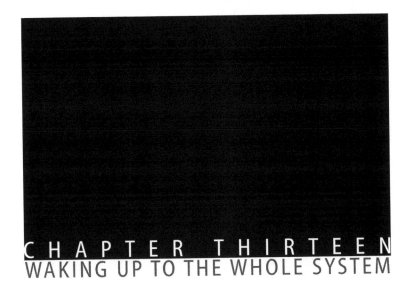

CHAPTER THIRTEEN
WAKING UP TO THE WHOLE SYSTEM

Miracles are a retelling in small letters the very same
story which is written across the whole world
in letters too large for some of us to see.

—C.S. Lewis

Hands-off success is enhanced by feeling your connection to everything. It comes from feeling all the support you are already getting.

You don't need to put your hands on anything to wring out that support. It's already everywhere. Almost a miracle.

Duane told me:

I had a friend challenge me once. He said, "Show me any-thing you possess that came to you solely from your own resources. The shirt on your back? Your belt? Your house? Your car? Anything!" I couldn't come up with anything,

145

even when I thought in terms of my physical body. My body came to me from my parents; I don't remember having done anything to put that together. I could not think of a single thing. Although I have done things to contribute to the manufacture of products, they all involved other people. I could not think of one single thing that was created solely and individually by myself. Even if I went out in the woods with a pocket knife and cut off a tree limb and carved something, it was contributed to me: the tree from nature and the knife by the knife manufacturer. I couldn't think of a thing.

Most people live completely unaware of how supported they are! They think they are relying on themselves. In their offices they have signs that say, "If it's to be, it's up to me."

They also think they can only make money if they take it from someone else. In their contracted view of life it's a zero-sum game. But the universe's evolution outward toward infinite expansion since the Big Bang is not a zero-sum game. And any time you try to create a system around the finite zero-sum premise, the system collapses, because it isn't in agreement with nature.

Marxism, just such a zero-sum system, was based on the paranoid concept of the finite limitation of wealth; in other words, there's only so much wealth in the world. It was the ultimate hands-*on* system of micromanagement taken to the extreme. Marxism holds that there are limited, finite resources and we must take these limited resources from the rich and redistribute them. What destroyed Marxism was the recognition in the free market system that wealth is infinite and unlimited. So, over in the Soviet system they kept redistributing their limited, finite amount of wealth, while in the Western free-market systems, wealth kept expanding. No wonder the socialist system collapsed and the Berlin Wall came tumbling down. The finite loses to the infinite every time.

The micromanager works with finite amounts of power and information, and the hands-off manager works with infinite imagination.

Wealth itself follows the path of a decidedly hands-off evolution and expansion, so that even "valueless" grains of sand have now been used to become the most valuable computer chips in the world.

To see the world in a grain of sand and to see heaven in a wild flower is to hold infinity in the palm of your hand and eternity in an hour.

—William Blake

And so, with imagination, resources are infinite, not finite. They're only limited by thought. They're not limited by the social structure you live in, as Karl Marx erroneously concluded. So the idea that *to have something, you must have taken it from someone else* is simply not in alignment with nature. And every time you try to put that idea out there as a system, the system collapses. Every time you try to follow it personally, your career suffers.

This limitation and finite thinking can also destroy an organization from within. For example, a lot of people think that if they deliver extraordinary customer service they'll have to give up something else: profit. They think that providing service the right way incurs an unnecessary expense. They don't have the imagination to see how huge a contribution great service is to their long-term bottom line.

And then they wonder why they're not successful in the long run.

To make certain you never fall into this zero-sum black hole, simply focus on what you're giving. Not on what you get back, nor on the results of giving or goals for the giving. Trust the system. Know that it will work. Because you are giving into an interconnected system. By doing this, you will get results.

The hands-off manager can enjoy keeping her hands off the process because she can see how big a process it really is. She can see how supported she is by good people everywhere. So she begins to function as a part of a whole, instead of being just a frightened, defensive individual.

Feeling that interconnection with everyone in your organization spreading forth to vendors and to customers, you realize that you get back what you give out, that what goes around, comes around, and that this hands-off mentoring style creates a circular path: The things you give out circulate through the world and come back to you.

The cynical person believes a capitalistic society functions because it promotes doing what's best for the individual even if it's at the expense of the whole. So if it's at the expense of the environment, that's okay, because you individually benefited. But then in the long run all of society has to pick up the tab for the damage that that particular individual or group did to the environment.

That cynical, individualistic approach is not going to work.

Each smallest act of kindness reverberates across great distances and spans of time, affecting lives unknown to the one whose generous spirit was the source of this good echo, because kindness is passed on and grows each time it's passed, until a simple courtesy becomes an act of selfless courage years later and far away.

—H.R. White

The higher your consciousness is, the more you can see the interconnectedness of all things. You see that it's not possible to damage the environment without damaging yourself. And people who try to accrue things without benefiting others end up as the Enron leaders did: dead or in jail. People who damage the environment, as in the case of the *Exxon Valdez* oil spill, damage themselves financially. And there's no way out of the connected web of life. There's no way to disconnect from the interconnectedness of all of life and the universe.

Is this too mystical? It's better described as *waking up to reality*. It's just waking up to the physical reality of the interconnectedness of all things. What it's waking up to is sometimes described as the "butterfly effect." We live by the butterfly effect in our company, whether we know it or not. (It's more fun when we know it.) What is the butterfly effect? Chaos theory states that something as small as the flutter of a butterfly's wing can ultimately cause a typhoon halfway around the world. If a butterfly in Peking flaps its wings it will affect the weather in Des Moines, Iowa, a week later.

In other words, there's no way anybody can do anything without affecting everything else.

When anyone in a business career or an organization wakes up to the butterfly effect, they start contributing all day to the higher good of the team. With everything they do. They face each challenge by asking themselves what they can contribute, rather than who they can blame.

Be sure you're really giving

Many people we have worked with think they are contributing when they are not. What they perceive as giving is actually a form of trading. They're always trying to calculate their return. Should I help this vendor? Should I help my coworker out of her jam? Should I refund the money to this customer? What would that bring back to me? Would that cut into my profits? Should I meet with this person from the other department to hear her complaint? What would I get back?

It's all a big trade-off to them. But trading is not giving. Giving has no ulterior motive. It is a way of being.

Think of your company as a mobile hanging from the ceiling. The whole web of the mobile is interconnected, so if you push on one part of it, you move all of it, even if just slightly.

When you are an ongoing contribution to your people and your customers, you never know what's coming back to you, and you don't have time to try to figure it out. Figuring it out is a waste of energy. With all the mental energy you're using trying to figure out your return, you could be doing more giving. And the one "unimportant" customer you treat badly could very well have potential to refer more people to you than you ever thought possible, and there's no way to figure out who that is ahead of time.

A business coach we were working with said, "Well, I gave my friend Joe a half-day of business coaching; he said he'd pay me when he could and he never paid me back, so that didn't work. Giving doesn't always work." And he never thought about the fact that six months later, another friend passed along a major client to him. He thought they were unrelated. We think too small. We don't realize that the person we're helping is very likely not the person we're going to get help back from. More often than not, we get it back from someone who has extra capacity to give to us. So the circle isn't just between you and one person; it's between you and everyone. You and the whole. Imagine the rungs on a ladder. You receive from the rung above you and you give to the one below you. Another way to say it is that you receive from those who have more and give to those who have less. In this context you don't expect to get back from the person you gave to, but you trust that the universe will give back to you in other ways from other sources.

We knew a salesperson named Stan. Stan was an incredible top salesperson who had just joined a new company we were training. The first thing he did when he got there was sit down with everybody inside that company one at a time to get to know them. He treated them like gold, no matter what their position. He found out what their jobs were and he asked them how he could help them in his sales role. How could he interact with them in a way that would be most beneficial to them? He got to know them. And other jealous salespeople saw him as a real charmer. But they didn't know why he was "wasting his time" with all those people in lower positions.

It's true that Stan was a manipulator. But a great pianist is a manipulator, too, when his fingers manipulate the piano keys to perform a beautiful sonata. Stan didn't have to try to work up some "trust" that everybody he was meeting with could someday help him. He didn't care. He knows the universe so well that he has a certainty about the interconnectedness of everything. He has a *certainty* that kindness to one person is never wasted, even if that specific person doesn't end up helping him in any way. He knows that his time is never wasted because it is a kindness invested into the system.

In the biographical movie *Gandhi*, when everyone around Gandhi was yelling about something the Jews were doing wrong, he stopped his followers and said, "I'm a Jew." They were stunned and didn't know what he meant. But his message finally sank in. What he meant was, don't pretend Jews are not connected to us. Don't make them separate. They are part of us.

Gandhi was trying to wake his followers up to a higher level of realization of the interconnectivity of everyone and everything.

Appreciation is a wonderful thing. It makes what
is excellent in others belong to us as well.

—Voltaire

Earlier in my career I joined with Michael Bassoff to create a very successful fundraising system called "RelationShift" fundraising. (Our book about it is *RelationShift: Revolutionary Fundraising*.) That system is based on shifting (actually, reversing) the relationship between the donor and the organization, so that the donor is appreciated in very large ways.

We have trained many nonprofit organizations in this system of giving more back to the donor than the donor gave them. Your gift to your donor is part of the interconnectedness of all spirit, no matter what. You can't not get it back. You can't break the system. We've proven this in our unorthodox fundraising system over and over, wherever it's been applied! You can't out-give the giver. You can't give somewhere and not get more back. You can't beat the system! It's a system that exists beyond trust and belief. For it to really flow and function you don't have to try to have faith in it. Let's take electricity. Most do not truly understand how it works; they just know that it does. You already know it works. And when you're a hands-off manager you don't have to try to work up "trust" or "faith" in the principle of ongoing contribution. You already know it works. You can keep contributing to the higher good of the organization and just let your career unfold.

It keeps life simple. Joy and bliss are not complicated; they come from simple acceptance.

Steps to hands-off success in your life

Three action steps to take after reading this chapter:

1. Don't hesitate to be of assistance to anyone and everyone in your organization. Too much time is wasted at work trying to decide whom to talk to.

2. Drop the distinction of "unimportant people" from your mindset. Every customer and every coworker has the power to advance your career beautifully, often in unseen and unknowable ways.

3. The next time another department or person is being criticized in a team meeting, stop the meeting and tell your team you are going to invite that person in to the next meeting so you can all talk together. Let other departments join your meetings often. Bring people together. Let everyone in the organization experience how interconnected they are.

CHAPTER FOURTEEN
DEEPENING YOUR DESIRES

Purpose and determination are not merely mental states. They have electrochemical connections that affect the immune system.

—Norman Cousins

The hands-off manager always wants to go deeper. He wants to find what lies beneath a coworker's desire. He doesn't just want to know what you want; he wants to know why you want it. That will tell him more about how he can help. Asking these questions will allow him to help someone not only realize their true desires, but see the underlying *sources* of those desires.

An employee may say, "I want to drive a Mercedes." And you, as a mentor, will go deeper and ask, "Why do you want a Mercedes?"

"I want to have very reliable, high-quality transportation."

"How else might you achieve that for yourself now, so it isn't left stranded out there in the future?"

Or maybe you're meeting with a new employee and talking about her career goals. She says, "I want to be rich."

That's a good start. But why?

She says, "I want to be secure so I don't have to worry about where my next dollar is coming from. I want to have enough money that I can be generous with others, and maybe give some money to charity." That is the deeper desire, and the one you can help her realize now.

One of the most effective methods a hands-off manager uses to bring out the best in employees is learning their deepest desires. Once you know what they are, you can put your mentoring and coaching into that context. You are helping them get what *they* want, not what *you* want.

And when you take their "wish list" deeper than the first blush, you can show them how to live the life they dreamed of right now, with your full support. Otherwise your people are seeking the end without the means. They'll be left stranded in their own futures with no one to pick them up and give them a ride home.

You will help them go right to the means. So instead of having goals about how many millions they're going to have, they now have intentions about how effective a person they're going to be. They now have intentions about what's inside them that would create the wealth.

Under your mentoring they can *reformat* their approach to what they want.

Wanting something is always coming from the position of weakness. To want something is to say "I'll probably never have it, but I wish I could." Wanting emphasizes its lack. So there's no self-esteem in it. There's no self-confidence built by wanting. It's like drowning your desires in fear-based hope.

Most people in the workplace are in this cloud of fearful hope. Your skill as a mentor will be to remove the cloud. You'll help them internalize and realize their purpose in each act of contribution, so that it doesn't live out there in an estranged future.

Nothing contributes so much to relax the mind as a steady purpose—a point on which the soul may fix its intellectual eye.

—Mary Shelley

Your team members then shift their purpose from things they want to ways they want to *be*. And paradoxically, they get things more quickly that way: Wealth flows into ways of being more quickly than it does into fits of wanting. Soon your career-direction meetings with your people shift their focus: Instead of traditional goals measured as successful by the CPAs or the tax code, you have created within your team a simple desire to make a difference.

You can apply this everywhere. You'll be asked to speak to a group of people, and rather than desiring to be a great speaker, you now just desire to make a connection with the group to whom you are talking. Connection is all you care about now. You can't be a speaker without a listener, so you've learned how to speak into the listening process.

I once taught a graduate program at the University of Santa Monica in presentation skills and public speaking. The first thing I said when I got up on the stage to teach my students was, "If I had only two words to teach you this semester, the two words I would use are these." I wrote on the white board "only connect." And I said, "That's all you're about, that's all you have to worry about, that's all you have to care about."

Some of the students asked if they could see a video of them speaking so that they would know what to improve. I said, "Wrong focus. If I were to make a video, I would have the video be of your audience, not you. Then we will sit and watch the audience. But we will not watch you. It's not about how you're coming across; it's about whether *they* feel a true connection to you."

When your direct reports want something, ask questions that take them deeper. What drives that desire? If somebody says, "I want to be famous," you might ask, "Why do you want to be famous?" And they might say in an unguarded moment, "Well, because famous people make a difference and people pay attention to them." And you ask, "Well, why don't you just make people pay attention to you by making a difference? Because right now you can make a difference. You don't have to wait to become famous. You have a desire that's been put in the future. But you could have it now."

You can lead people away from their weakest position— *Gee, I wish I could have what I want...but I'll probably never get there*—and lead them into giving away what they want! If they want appreciation, they can give more away. Soon, whenever they even think of something they want, they can say to themselves, *I'm just going to give it away!* After they practice doing that for a while, they begin to realize, *If I have it to give away, I must already have it!*

Follow effective action with quiet reflection. From the
quiet reflection will come even more effective action.

—Peter Drucker

Steps to hands-off success in your life

Three action steps to take after reading this chapter:

1. Write down the four material things you want most in life right now. Boat, house, entertainment system, car, whatever. Leave plenty of space below what you wrote down.
2. Now write down why you want it: for example, "It would give me...." or, "It would mean that...." Discover the ways of being those "things" would create for you.
3. Finally, imagine how you can be that way right now. Today. At work and at home. Once you practice this act of deepening your desires and seeing what lies beneath each one, you can meet with each employee on your team and talk about their big picture career desires. You'll help them get to their own way of being that they're not yet giving themselves permission to understand. As a gifted hands-off mentor you will be able to show them that their best nature was being held hostage by an uncertain future. That they were saving their best for some yet-to-be realized experience. By showing them this, you will free them to be who they always wanted to be, now.

CHAPTER FIFTEEN
LIVING IN THREE WORLDS

The greatest natural resource in the world is not in the Earth's
waters or minerals, nor in the forests or grasslands. It is the
spirit that resides in every unstoppable person.

—Cynthia Kersey

I recently coached a business owner named Milo who had a
large team of salespeople in the real estate field. He kept talking
about how hard it was to get real producers on his sales team and
keep them there.

He talked about the volatile market, the attitude of young
people today, and the poor hiring system in his HR department.
These were outer manifestations of his own scarcity thinking—his
erroneous belief that he never has enough of anything.

"What do you want?"

"An all-star team of producers, instead of this high-turnover joke of a team I've got."

"Then create it," I said.

"What do you mean by that?"

"Build it. Stop wishing for it. That will push it away. Start building it."

Milo took a long time, but he finally began to see that he could build his team from within. He let all his company members participate in recruiting. He changed his compensation system so people had higher incentives to stay a long time. Then everything began changing from within.

Milo soon realized the insanity of trying to fix what had already happened. Why try to undo history? You can't do that. It was time to let it go and dive back inside. To connect with his inner spirit, the only true leverage point for change.

Success comes from three worlds

Allowing success requires that we create an understanding within ourselves of the existence of three worlds. Worlds that we live in every moment of every day, simultaneously. These worlds are spirit, mind, and body (or the physical world). And you can't actually see most of what happens in those three worlds.

Duane explained his theory of three worlds one warm Sunday morning in his home while my tape recorder was running. He produced a diagram he had made (see the end of this chapter) to illustrate his point, and said, "If you've ever seen a scientific analysis of the spectrum of visible light, all the way from infrared down to real slow waves, there's only a little tiny sector in the middle that's visible. And it represents a very small percentage of what's actually coming at us. Our whole lives are like that spectrum."

"How do you mean?"

"We have three worlds that exist in us simultaneously at all times. And the important thing to understand about these worlds is where the power really lies. Where the potential for success in life is located. It's not in the physical world, as we all assume it is."

Duane explained that we spend most of our time focused on the physical world. But the physical world is just the manifestation of what has been created in the inner two worlds. By the time you see it, it's too late to change anything.

"Because the physical world is nothing more than manifest destiny," he said. "The real change happens internally, not externally. Change only becomes *visible* in the external world."

So our ability to make a difference and change the results we're seeing does not happen by focusing on and fixing external events. Our access to destiny occurs earlier in the process than that. It occurs when we focus on spirit (our intuition and inspiration) and mind (our thinking and planning). That's the only domain where we can exercise free will and free choice.

"You don't get to choose whether the sun's going to come up tomorrow." said Duane. "Nor do you get to choose how other people are going to behave or react to a given circumstance. But you do get to choose *who you are being.*"

Our behavior is nothing more than a reflection of our inner way of being.

"So if you think you can control your behavior without altering your inner being, you're living in a dream world, not in the world of reality."

Employee surveys will confirm it

Notice that all the employee surveys that show people's dislike of being "micromanaged" and "distrusted" and "not communicated with" reflect the manager's misguided and ill-chosen attempts to manage things that have already happened. The second-guessing and criticism runs rampant through the workplace because the manager is not operating at the source.

Hands-off managers know all three worlds and, therefore, become masters of mind and spirit, as well. They know that the world of spirit is universal. It's an interconnectedness of everyone and all things. It has unlimited potential.

Duane explained to me that the world of the mind is another world inside us: It's our thinking and our beliefs. It's our fears (generally caused by judgments) and anything we've incorporated into our thought process.

Our negative thoughts are the very things we should be working on clearing out so that more of our potential can come through.

"And then there's the physical world," Duane said as he pointed to the "physical world" section of his diagram. "This is going to sound strange, but it's an imaginary world."

"In what way?"

"It is made up of images!"

The Native Americans were once criticized because they believed their waking hours were imaginary and their dreams were real. Consider that this may not have been too far from the truth, because what we see is not really what has happened. It's only how things have come together in the end.

This has been referred to as the Iceberg Principle.

The Iceberg Principle would say that what you see above the surface in the ocean when you look at an iceberg is only about 10 percent of the entire iceberg. The other 90 percent of the ice floats below the surface and is not visible to the eye.

"That's exactly what's occurring in our own world,"

"That's exactly what's occurring in our own world," Duane said. "What we see coming through in physical form is a very tiny portion of all that's actually happening."

Duane added the metaphor of electricity to illustrate his point. He recalled an electrician friend who went to the Middle East as part of a job. His friend was trying to teach people in a remote village to run electrical wiring in their houses. Duane said:

You know how we hide wires in the walls here? He couldn't do that there. They wouldn't accept it. They wouldn't believe that a light switch that had no visible connection to a light at the top of the room would ever be able to turn it on and off. It was inconceivable to them that that was possible, even when he showed them how to do it! As soon as he covered it up with drywall or plaster or some sort of surfacing material, they would not accept that it would be possible. They would think it was dark magic. And so my friend had to rethink how he taught people to install electricity in their house, because they could not do it in the American format; it was unacceptable to these people.

We may be surprised at the ignorance of those people. "But we are equally ignorant," said Duane, "about something more important than wires in walls. About the spectrum of life itself."

We think the world outside us is the only real world. Because all we're really seeing is the world of manifestation. We don't understand how that world was created and the influence we have over the 90 percent of what we don't see.

The world of concept, which is contained in the world of spirit, and the world of creation, which is contained in the world of mind, facilitate and create what is manifest in the physical world. So by the time anything happens in the physical world, it's out of our control. Do you notice that in the workplace?

By the time a new system for sales commissions is implemented, the all-too-common negative reaction to change is happening and the push-back is the new problem. The influence and impact we might have had on acceptance of the system has already been undermined in the other two worlds by people's belief that change is bad! The physical world is just the end product.

The hands-off manager will say, "Focus on the process, not the results." The process is the mind and the spirit inside. It's the heart of your organization. If you focus on the process, the results will unfold naturally from that. So if you have an inner process that creates a quality sales force, good customer service, a reliable product, and a good marketing plan, you don't have to worry about how to be successful. It flows easily into fruition from that. The creative work has already been done.

The difficulty arises when you *don't* have those ingredients and you try to produce an outcome anyway. It's similar to trying to bake a cake with no recipe and no ingredients and still expecting it to come out delicious.

You can't get there from nothing.

The hands-off manager sets himself apart by understanding the creative process and shifting the focus of his energy and attention to where he *can* make a difference. You can do this, too. You can shift your attention to your own thinking. That's where you can have an impact on what shows up in your life and what shows up in the world.

> The sword and the spirit are the two mightiest forces in the world. Yet the spirit is mightier of the two.
>
> —Napoleon Bonaparte

The spiritual world is the world of essence. It's that part of you that you're learning to bring through. It's the best of who you are, your higher self, and your most unlimited potential.

The mind is the world of the ego. Your ego has value because it identifies you as an individual and gives you access to your unique experience. Ego individuates you and brings your experience of being a singular being in physical form.

The physical world is just the world of activity. It's the world in which you can joyfully follow through on and act out the part you've created internally.

The world of spirit is the world of possibility. The mental world is the world of choices. The physical world is the world of destiny.

So now you can begin to focus on where you can really cause change. If you want to make a change, it starts in the worlds of mind and spirit. Your spiritual world becomes the world in which ideas, inspiration, and insights originate. When you have an open mind that is free of judgment and expectation, you receive at a much higher level. The mental world is where you create plans; it's the world where you use thought, analysis, focus, and attention to bring into being that which you desire to contribute to the world.

The physical world is just the world of events, of information. It's where results occur, where data is collected, where the object is manifest, where the outcome happens, and where the action takes place. It's the last stage of the process.

Walter owned a small manufacturing company trying to produce a better product. He was old-school and full of fear. So his approach was to simply get angry about the customer response to the product he now had. But he was making no changes in his assembly line. He didn't understand that you can't change a result without changing the ingredients that went into producing the result. The true ingredients that create the result are contained in the world inside you, not in the world outside you.

Walter finally sold his business at a great loss. If you truly want to make a difference, you focus on your inner systems because that's where you have power. You don't just focus on what's happened in the world. All that does is act like a mirror; it reflects back to you what you've been thinking. Duane says:

> I try to communicate to people an understanding that experience is not final truth. And they really have a hard time with that. I say, "All experience tells you is what you've been thinking. It tells you the results of the beliefs and ways of thinking you've had in the past. That's what experience tells you. It doesn't tell you what's true. Just because you failed at this once, doesn't mean you have to fail at it again. It means you never believed you could succeed, and therefore you have manifested exactly what you believed."

Life will not bring you what you want. Life will bring you what you believe. Wanting it actually pushes it away!

And the reason it does is that *wanting it* creates a belief that *you don't have it*, and that maybe you can't get it. It creates inner lack and a sense of scarcity regarding that subject.

So how can you stop wanting something you really want?

Instead of wanting it, you can shift your thinking to, "I'll create it." Because you now understand that the true creative process begins on the inside, not the outside. You comprehend that the creative potential that exists within you comes through your thinking, which arises through what's in you. It's an inside job.

> Man must evolve for all human conflict a method
> which rejects revenge, aggression, and retaliation.
> The foundation of such a method is love.
>
> —Dr. Martin Luther King, Jr.

One of the best examples of using all three worlds as opposed to just one, is contained in a comparison of the lives of Malcolm X and Dr. Martin Luther King, Jr.

Malcolm X tried to erase already-existing racism. His whole approach was that racism is bad, it's wrong, and we need to get rid of it. He was trying, through his justifiable anger, to alter the already-existing physical world. So he wasn't in three worlds, he was in one. He kept trying to chop off the tip of the iceberg.

Dr. Martin Luther King, Jr., approached the issue differently. He went inside himself to the level of spirit. He was a minister who knew how to meditate and pray for inspiration. Finally, when it arrived, he said to the world, "I have a dream."

Dr. King's dream had black people and white people going to the same schools and the same restaurants, and being treated equally by the law. That was his dream. He didn't talk about racism in his dream, because racism was history to him. And in his dream racism would no longer be relevant.

So now we celebrate a holiday in his honor. There isn't a holiday for Malcolm X. Despite his courage and brilliance, Malcom X has had very little lasting influence. His time on earth did more to fuel the anger of his followers than it did to create anything new.

But because of King, a lot is different now; he found his leverage at the level of a dream, at the level of an idea, instead of the level of outer historical manifestation. He was accessing spirit, not physical form. King exemplifies someone who goes into his inner world of the spiritual to adjust something in the outer world—as opposed to the way most of us handle life: complaining about what's already out there.

If you look at the people who have truly influenced the world, they were always inner-idea people. They include such notables as Gandhi; Thomas Edison; Joan of Arc; Martin Luther King, Jr.; Christ; Buddha; and the list goes on. They influenced our thinking, our philosophies, and our beliefs. They shifted the world. They changed the course of history, and they used an understanding of the three worlds to do it.

To realize your full potential, all you have to do is focus on the ingredients. Look inside to change the inner process, and just let the results happen. Let your process produce the results that it will naturally. Soon you will learn to make a difference. You'll become a person of real influence. You'll become a person who significantly alters what happens in the physical world as a result of your having been here.

The Declaration of Independence was a document about a new way of being, a new governance. Our Constitution was an idea. Both of these ideas came from inspired people who connected to their potential and utilized all three worlds to bring forth their ideas.

As a result of Enron and other newsworthy corporate transgressions, our government is trying hard to control business and public corporations from the outside. To force them through all sorts of exercises, procedures, documentation, and additional audit processes to keep them from taking advantage of people. But change happens from within. Companies that don't exploit people have already had the idea not to. They have just adopted the idea that they do not want to take advantage of people. They have become people whose true desire is to do what is best.

We are always trying to fix what's wrong instead of finding what's possible. Fixing never really works. If anything, it makes the problem worse. The Resolution Trust Corporation—the U.S. government–owned asset management company mandated to liquidate the assets of insolvent savings and loan companies—often spent more money on legal pursuits and resolving the so-called problems of the institutions than they received from selling all of their assets. This whole governmental "fixing" was a complete disaster. It wasn't a failure of the institutions as much as it was a failure of government policy. It's a graphic example of how trying to change a result that's already occurred isn't going to change anything.

Only coming up with a whole new system will ever truly affect the outcome. One simply must focus on what could be, rather than what has been.

When you observe children on a playground, almost nothing makes them more spirited and inspired than when one of the kids stands up and says, "Hey, I've got an idea!" And everybody comes alive.

"Oh, what?"

And the kid says, "Let's build a tree fort!"

"Yes!"

They're actually using all three worlds: the first world is the spirit, the inspiration ("I've got an idea!"); the second world is the mind ("Let's build a tree fort!"); and the third world is the physical manifestation, the actual tree fort. There's nothing more inspiring than a fresh idea. That's how tree forts get built. Because everybody gets inspired by the idea, and the tree fort is what you see at the end.

What happens in most workplaces is that everybody walks around grumbling because there isn't a tree fort, and there isn't a good compensation plan, and the IT system's software isn't right—all the focus is on the physical world, which is always perceived to be inadequate. They focus on what they have already manifested, instead of the fresh idea that would change everything.

Most micromanagers we work with are so busy trying to repair the already-sinking Titanic that they can't sit still for this teaching. "Spirit?" they say. "I'm dealing with real world problems here! Go back to California!" But this is exactly the insight they need. Knowing about and utilizing all three worlds would change everything for them.

When the world of quantum physics expanded people's minds, it lifted the world out of the old-school Newtonian cause-and-effect belief system. It disproved the crudely mechanical explanations of infinite, creative time and space. It opened the mind.

It's time the workplace had the same open-minded revolution.

Take a look at Duane's chart on the next page as a reminder of how the three worlds inside us relate to each other. Note that intuition is the mind's link to the world of spirit, and the five senses are the mind's link to the physical world. Everything that is happening in our lives is experienced through our judgments, attitudes, and beliefs, and the mind is the controlling factor. It is the bridge between concept and manifestation.

The creative process—understanding all three worlds. Most of what is happening is unseen.

Intuition and the five senses are the links between the three worlds.

SPIRITUAL		MENTAL		PHYSICAL
Spirit		Mind		Body
			F	
Universal	I	Individual	I	Imaginary
Concept	N	Creation	V	Manifestation
Essence	T	Ego	E	Activity
Possibility	U	Choice		Destiny
Understanding	I	Experience	S	Events
Wisdom	T	Knowledge	E	Information
Idea	I	Thought	N	Result
Knowing	O	Opinion	S	Data
Insight	N	Analysis	E	Object
Inspiration		Focus	S	Outcome

Potential　　　**Attention**　　　**Action**

Steps to hands-off success in your life

Three action steps to take after reading this chapter:

1. List three things in the outer world of the workplace you don't like. Three systems or situations you wish were different.
2. Under each item write the words "spirit," "mind," and "body."
3. Trace each manifestation back to its original impulse (spirit)—what was it initially thought to accomplish?—and then trace it to Mind (the thoughts and plans that went into it) and see if you can come up with new systems.

CHAPTER SIXTEEN
THE HANDS-OFF MANAGER AS COACH

*Our chief want in life is to find someone
who will make us do what we can.*

—Ralph Waldo Emerson

Morale in the workplace is the creation of the leader. He or she coaches it into existence. Or doesn't. But morale is not just an accidental climate that comes in on the wind.

A manager we'll call Tony was a gifted project manager who oversaw construction sites for Duane many years ago. His skills and intellect were exceptional, but Tony was not happy in his work.

Two upper managers who came to review Tony's progress in monthly update meetings were relentlessly critical and questioning of Tony's decisions, and Tony was too sensitive a person to let it go.

The quality of his work began to deteriorate to levels that were unacceptable. He justified his shortcomings by saying that these two managers were interfering with his well-being. He couldn't stand the criticism.

Finally, Duane had had enough. He knew that compassionate listening had run its course, and it was time to upgrade the coaching to the tough-love level.

"Tony, I want to ask you a question," Duane said.

Tony said nothing.

"Has there ever been a time when these two managers' comments were deliberately designed to hurt you and undermine your work?"

"No," Tony said, after some hesitation.

Duane continued, "Has there ever been anything they have communicated to you that wasn't intended to make you more successful at getting the job done?"

"I suppose not, no," said Tony.

"So it's a matter of style, then," said Duane. "You are reacting emotionally, not to what they are communicating, but the way in which they say the words."

"If you put it that way, I guess I am."

"Then I'm going to ask you for something. I'm going to ask you to grow up. I'm going to ask you to learn a more mature way to reformat what they are saying so that you can hear it as support and not as a threat to you."

"I don't know…." said Tony.

"Because it is support, Tony, and they just don't know how to communicate with you in a way that considers your sensitivity to criticism."

Tony was quiet.

"Tony," Duane said, "today is Thursday. I want you to take the rest of the week off and do whatever it is you do to help you make a big decision. Then Monday we will meet and discuss your future with this company. You are capable of far better work than you are producing. If you find you are unwilling to grow up and take their communication gracefully, I'm going to let you go. I have no desire to have someone as capable as you are be this unhappy."

Tony came in Monday with a huge smile on his face.

Duane asked him what decision he had made.

"I'm excited," Tony said. "I never saw my own part in this. I never realized that I could reformat this. I really think you have changed my life."

As the months and years rolled along, Tony came to Duane many more times to thank him for that fateful meeting and for changing his life. He told Duane that he was one of the most influential people in his life. This ended up being an incredibly positive experience for Tony. Learning to deal with the two critical managers had, in fact, provided him with a great service. It helped him grow up.

The thing we surrender to becomes our power.

—Ernest Holmes

Do people really change?

I get that question all the time in my leadership seminars. But asking the question itself betrays a lack of understanding of human nature.

People do nothing *but* change. Sometimes for the better, sometimes for the worse. But it's in the nature of a human being to be ever-changing. Every living thing is always changing, so why would we humans be any different?

Yet we think we are! We think people have permanent, fixed personalities that they are all stuck with. Especially in the workplace. People get labeled early on and are dealt with based on the label. This is a mistake.

Can you coach another person so that the person really changes?

We saw how Duane coached Tony. That's one example that confirms it can be done, but let's look at another example. Let's look at the example of me. Let's examine the notion that people never change through the sample of this one life of mine.

If you saw a man who used to be drunk most of the time—a young man whose life was nothing much more than lying, cheating, stealing, drug-taking, drinking, and running up a massive debt—you would have a hard time trusting, or even liking, that man. But what if you saw that same man today and he had not had a drink or drug in 26 years, was happy and healthy with a wonderful family and fulfilling successful career dedicated to helping other people? Would you call that a change?

Every person on the planet today who has transformed from the low, suicidal life of addiction to a new life of spirit, service, and health—and there are millions of them!—has more than "changed." They have become someone else. They have become their potential.

And, in most cases, they have been coached.

Sometimes coaching takes on the form of parenting. Sometimes it shows up as 12-step sponsorship, and sometimes it is just sharing an idea with a friend. But one thing is certain: people can change—and coaching can accelerate that change.

My first sponsor in my 12-step program coached me from the living suicide of drinking and addiction to higher levels of life than I ever dreamed possible. We worked with a book (most coaches are very intimate with transformative books) and we charted a new path for my life.

Once I'd reached a (blessed) level of clarity and sobriety, my mind was open to even more coaching from books and then from more mentors. (Spiritual growth has no upper limit. Just when you think you're as happy as a person can be, it gets better.) The coaching I received took me from abject financial disaster to a successful professional career.

Yet when we think about coaching, especially "life coaching," we sometimes think of ineffective, New Age-y, faux guru types who sit with their clients and channel spirit beings. And that doesn't sound like something that would be a good fit for a high-powered organization that really wants to move numbers forward and achieve proactive success.

But good coaching does just that. In fact, the word coaching comes from the world of sports. A world of performance and numbers. Therefore, sports provides a perfect metaphor for what good coaching is in an organization. The first thing a masterful coach does is decrease the fearful emotional charge inside the person being coached. As the great football coach Vince Lombardi said, "It's hard to be aggressive when you're confused." So, if you're coaching me, you first bring your positive attention to my situation. Soon my negative feelings start to lift. I was working with a large group of managers one day when Duane Black himself volunteered to step to the front of the room to illustrate a point I was making. He walked up to the two flip-charts I was using to contrast the thinking of ownership versus the thinking of victimization.

"Let's try looking at it this way," Duane said going to the ownership flip-chart. He drew a very large plus sign on the page and said, "When you are positive (pointing to the sign), you add something to any situation, conversation, or meeting you are in. That's what being positive does, it contributes. It adds something."

He then walked over to the victim's flip chart, drew a large minus sign, and said, "When you are negative, you subtract something from the conversation, the meeting, or the relationship. If you are negative often enough, you subtract so much from the relationship that there is no more relationship."

Duane was giving us the simple math of the human interactive experience! It was a law of the universe up there on the flip-chart of life: positive adds, negative subtracts. A positive person contributes, a negative person takes away. I immediately recalled that in grade school, the minus sign was called the "take-away" sign.

As in math, when you introduce a negative to the workplace, it diminishes the total. Add a negative person to the team and the energy of the team is diminished.

When you are a positive leader with positive thoughts about the future and the people you lead, you add something to every person you talk to. You bring something of value to every communication. Every e-mail and voicemail that's positive adds something to the life of the person who receives it. Because positive always adds to (increases, improves) something.

It's a definite plus.

It runs even deeper than that. If you think positive thoughts throughout the day, you are adding to (plus sign) your own deep inner experience of living. You are bringing a plus to your own spirit and energy with each positive thought.

Your negative thoughts take away (minus sign) from the experience of being alive. They rob you of your energy.

And so the first thing a coaching conversation does is change the math. It alters the charge in the mind of the person being coached from negative to positive. That alone makes coaching immediately valuable.

Notice that most hands-on old-school micromanagers almost always bring a negative charge to their human interaction throughout the day. Every time they indulge in sarcasm about the organization, skepticism about the mission, or cynicism about the customer, the negativity builds. And they do this all day long.

One of the Internet's most successful business gurus is Matt Furey (*www.mattfurey.com*), a former international champion martial artist who specializes in coaching his clients to stunning financial results. He is a friend of mine and shared with me his own thoughts about negative people and the message he likes to send.

"If you're interested in more success," says Matt, "then you and I can spend time together. If you're interested in blaming others, staying stuck, whining, complaining, and so on, then we will not hang out together. Simple as that. Now, why do you think I have this rule? I have it because I have witnessed what happens to me when I am around successful people. I get charged up. I get excited. And I succeed even more than before. But if I hang out with people who act and think like losers, then I start going downhill."

A client of mine I'll call Linda had a real problem. She was trying to run a sales and marketing team and failing at every turn. She was selling a service targeted to women, and her team was comprised of women who loved and admired Linda—almost to the point of worship.

Linda's product was wonderful, but her team was losing money, and when she hired me to coach her, she thought she was a hands-off manager, but she wasn't.

Linda had the same misconception about hands-off management that many people do—they think it means no accountability. They think it means to just fire people up, love them and then look the other way. If they don't perform, express your hurt and disappointment.

Dangerous misconception.

Dangerous because you can lose your business or have your team fail miserably thinking this way.

Linda didn't realize it, but she was trying to run her team on emotion alone. If her people had a bad month, she would get angry and subtly intimidate them. If they had a good month, she would become overjoyed and take them all out to a champagne dinner filled with promises and mindless joy.

When we sat down together for our first session, I wanted to have Linda see the importance of accountability.

"Business is a logical process run by emotional beings," I told her, paraphrasing my favorite small-business millionaire Sam Beckford.

"How does that apply to our team?" she asked.

"Your team is on a roller coaster, up one day and down the other, based on your mood. You are teaching your people that their only real job is to win your approval."

"Well, yes, that's right. I want them to sell more and know that I'll approve of them for that."

"Not logical," I said.

"How do you mean?"

"You're basing the mission on emotion. They can't perform well if they are constantly trying to anticipate your mood. That takes them back to dysfunction. Like little girls living in a household with an alcoholic mother. No one knows when it's safe to talk to Mother."

"What's the alternative?" she said.

I told her that the alternative was to return her people to their work. To let them love their work, and make it better every day. To measure their progress. But not to strike fear into their hearts.

Linda was stunned by my assessment of her leadership style, but as I worked with her she began to see the value of holding her people accountable to themselves and their own best possible performance. She was opening up to a new way of seeing her business. She hadn't always been this open!

"Why do I need coaching?" she once asked. "Why can't I be fiercely self-reliant?"

This myth of isolation is just about the most painful thing any of us experiences—all day thinking, *I'm all alone—lost and afraid in a world I never made.*

Reaching out for help is not weakness, it is the ultimate in strength. It is a commitment to something other than looking strong. It is a commitment to something beautiful, a mission beyond the ego.

Doctors coach us on how to get well, teachers coach us on how to become knowledgeable, parents coach us on how to grow up, so why is this not just the most beautiful, natural way of it? Why is this not the most powerful way to grow?

It's certainly the fastest.

Which is why the hands-off manager learns to become a masterful coach.

The great business management author and advisor Tom Peters says the manager in today's workplace cannot be like yesterday's boss. He tells managers, "Stop giving orders. Being the boss is no longer—if it ever was—about issuing mandates from on high. 'Ordering' change is a (stupid, stupid, stupid) waste of time."

Your own humility will allow you to win the support of your people. Because you value them at the same level that you value yourself. Humility is not low self-esteem—quite the opposite: humility is exceptionally high self-esteem. It demonstrates a self-confidence that is so unshakable that you never have to put someone else down in order to make yourself feel better.

Coaching that helps bring a person "into alignment" with their true talent (passion) is not some goofy New Age narcissism. It increases productivity; hard numbers and profitability are affected. The growth curve and real dollar profit margins of the company Duane works for can only astonish competitors and onlookers who are reduced to guessing that they must have made some lucky land acquisitions in a prime market with good timing.

Well, yes, timing is everything. Especially when we notice that the time is always now.

What to do when coaching doesn't work

If you have an unhappy employee who is under-producing, coaching is always your first option. Coaching can do so much!

Except when it can't.

Yes, there are times when even the most masterful coaching will not change an employee's poor attitude and inconsistent performance. Some people are just not open to it.

It is at this point that we like to remember the words of Harvey Mackay, chairman of the Mackay Envelope Company, who said, "It's not the people you fire who give you problems; it's the people you don't fire."

So why are we so reluctant to fire people? Aside from the paperwork annoyances involved, we are traumatized by the thought of firing someone for two very unnecessary reasons: (1) we think replacing them will be difficult, and (2) we think we will be doing them great harm.

Let's look at the first mental obstacle—the difficulty in replacing a person. The truly masterful hands-off manager must be a (not good, but) great recruiter and attractor of talent. Talent is everything today. The company with the most talent wins. Hands-off management is wasted on mediocre people. You want dedicated people who love what they do, and you want to be great at bringing them on board. So releasing a person who is unhappy and underperforming and not a team fit is a pleasure—not a problem. It is a pleasure because of who you have waiting in the wings! You are always making your team better and better. You understand that talent rules. It is not that you are always looking to replace and upgrade people who work for you. The opposite is true—you are constantly looking for ways to help them succeed. And a big part of that commitment to their success is the willingness to remove obstacles in their path. Sometimes those obstacles are people on the team who are simply not a fit—people who are not aligned with what the team is committed to.

The second mental obstacle is that thought that you are harming someone by firing them. You are not. If that person is unhappy and unproductive, you are harming them by keeping them. Letting them go will set them free to find work they like to do. In the end, that's the greatest gift you can give. Even current HR surveys show that people who are fired are more likely to improve their financial standing in life than people who quit. That's the proven career value of a wake-up call!

Football coach Vince Lombardi was famous for saying, "If you are not fired with enthusiasm, you will be fired with enthusiasm."

Duane lets people go who won't contribute and are misaligned with the team. He lets them go! He says to them, "You're my friend. I really care about you—and you're in the wrong position. You will be much happier when you find a job that you love to do. Even if you feel disappointed right now that I'm letting you go, even if you're angry, I still want you to have an opportunity to find alignment for yourself somewhere in a job that works for you. You're the right person for that. This is the wrong job for you."

Duane says that through the many years of working in his company he and his colleagues are unanimous on one point—"We've never let a person go too soon."

It's hard to keep creating a better team. We get distracted from the challenge by the daily problems of the workplace. Soon we think we're too pressed and swamped to recruit and interview properly so we hire people quickly to "fill immediate needs," and the quality of the team goes downhill. We have become distracted from our original vision. Therefore, vision-renewal is a daily activity of the hands-off manager. There can't be exceptions to the vision of excellence.

"You have to release people who are not right for the team," says Duane. "Because you care for them in a more elevated way than just trying to please them or be their buddy. You can't let the rest of your team suffer because of that one person. You end up working through a fair amount of people before you get the team you want, but once you do, they'll serve you for a long time. It's not like a sports team where athletes have short careers. Bodies wear down. But the mind lasts for a very long time."

Under the supervision of a hands-off manager, the mind grows stronger, more imaginative, and more excited about doing great work.

Mariano was a powerful CFO of a company with a good-sized accounting staff. He had been on my Website reading about the breakthroughs that hands-off management was achieving.

"I don't agree with your theories at all," he said, as we sat down to chat at an outdoor restaurant.

"Really?"

"Really," he said. "In fact, I told my partner that I was angry with you after reading your theories about hands-off guidance or whatever it is."

"That is okay with me," I said, "but remember that they're not theories. They are experience. You don't need theories about success in the workplace; there's enough actual experience to look at."

"Well, whatever—I got angry because I know it wouldn't work. I could never trust my people that much."

Mariano had always had problems with his people. He hired people in a hurry to meet needs and then spent most of his time furious with the mediocre work coming from his people.

"I have mediocre people," he said, "who need to be watched and monitored every minute."

"They are not mediocre people," I said. "In the right job, with a trusting mentor, they could be magnificent. Every last one of them."

"So you say."

Mariano was not a respecter of human talent although he himself had a great deal of it. To him, people basically weren't trustworthy, so therefore his recruiting efforts were never very visionary or creative. He always hired to fill a need. Never to fill a desire or to fulfill a vision.

Mariano's anger came from not knowing how to mentor people and allow them to be successful. He thought mentoring was weak. Especially compared to his own system of criticizing, correcting, humiliating, and embarrassing his people.

"Your system is too easy," he said.

"You were a parent raising your son for many years, if I am correct," I said.

Mariano nodded and said, "Oh, yes."

"Was that easy?"

"Hardest thing I've ever done."

"But you loved him."

"More than anything."

"And you guided him and mentored him."

"Constantly, until I didn't need to."

"Rewarding?"

"Oh, yes."

"And because of your love, was parenting a weak or soft activity?"

"I see where you're going with this, but there's no comparison."

"Why not?"

"You don't want me to all of a sudden love my employees like I love Derek?"

"Maybe not all of a sudden."

"After when? I get a heart transplant? After I get new employees?"

"After you coach them. After you really, truly coach them, you won't have to try to love them. It will just happen."

"Why is that?"

"Because you'll get closer with every session. You'll be partnering for the higher good. You'll be sharing life's most difficult experiences. And you'll be sharing life's best moments—moments of growth."

Mariano wasn't convinced. But he was willing to listen. And, ironically, he'd always been an admirer of Duane's team. ("How does he pull down those numbers year after year?" he would ask, shaking his head at this strange "magic.")

I wanted Mariano to get something: When firing a non-producer is not your current choice, then coaching is what you must do.

Seem obvious?

Not to Mariano! And not to most managers. Most managers know nothing of coaching. When a person underperforms, they don't coach them; they do other things, all of them toxic and dysfunctional. They become sarcastic. Or they ignore their employee, playing the time-worn game of "Guess Why I'm Mad." They reduce the logical process of business into an emotional battleground. Tension fills the workplace. Morale suffers.

"I don't know what else to do!" an angry CEO named Mark said when I talked to him about a team leader who wasn't getting the job done. "I'm caught between a rock and a hard place! I am furious with Gordon, but the nightmare of finding a replacement is too much to think about."

"How do you think he feels?" I asked.

"Frankly, that doesn't concern me right now, he has totally betrayed me." This was getting to be like a scene out of *General Hospital* for me, so I looked for a way to introduce coaching as an alternative to the daily drama.

"Have you ever coached him?" I asked. "Have you ever mentored Gordon?" Mark stared at me like I'd asked him whether he'd ever given him a pedicure. His face was twisted with confusion.

"What do you mean by coaching?" That was a valid question! What is this coaching process we're talking about? What do we do, exactly, when we coach someone?

Stop giving unsolicited advice.

A lot of people think that coaching means giving advice; that you give advice in kind of a nice way so that you're giving advice but you can call it "coaching." That's not really coaching. That's advising.

When you are coaching, the first thing you do is seek to understand the other person. You do not first seek to be understood. Understand where your person's heart is. What are they thinking? How do they see things? Because if you saw life the way they saw life, you'd likely be doing just what they're doing. You'd be behaving the way they were. You'd be communicating exactly the way they are. You'd be them.

It's really important for you to see what your people want to achieve and how they see their situation. Ask questions and let them talk. Keep your hands off their answers.

Grant that I may not so much seek to be consoled as to console; to be understood, as to understand; to be loved, as to love; for it is in giving that we receive.

—St. Francis of Assisi

In the old model of managing, people tried to be understood, period. End of communication! They had all their communications going out and nothing coming in. They were thinking, *I sure hope I'm being understood!* And then if somebody was messing up, that micromanager would sit down with them and say, "Let me tell you what you're doing wrong," or "Let me tell you what I expect of you, here."

And it wasn't working.

In today's organization the young people being hired are much brighter and more knowledgeable than ever before. But what comes along with that? They're also more independent and personally complex than ever before. They're not going to fall in line like people on the assembly line in the 1940s and just follow the orders being barked out and move like sheep through the organization.

About a decade ago, I worked for a company called TimeMax. We delivered productivity training and sold time-management products. Our company was struggling financially when it brought in a business coach by the name of Steve Hardison.

Hardison was dynamic. His coaching went through the company like a hurricane and it wasn't long before empty classrooms were converted to "standing room only," and major Fortune 500 companies were writing six-figure checks for our training.

Hardison's coaching sessions opened people up to levels of performance and creativity they never knew existed. I'd never seen anything like it.

And the best part of the company transformation was that it included me.

Not since I'd transformed from a hopelessly addicted person to a happy, clean and sober person had I changed so much.

Do people change?

Because of Hardison, I started teaching classes, giving seminars (I'd previously had a public speaking phobia), and writing books. I was 49 and had never written a book before. I've now written 16—some of them bestsellers. So, do people change? Does coaching work?

More than anyone can imagine!

"But you've got to have someone willing to receive," says Hardison. "Coaching can't be imposed from one person to another. It's a two-way street. It's an exchange of life. Both people learn. Both people grow."

Hardison has now coached some of the top celebrities in the entertainment industry and personal growth field and says that everyone's "problems" are the same.

"There's no new problem," Hardison said. "People are afraid to really express who they are. That's all that's going on. My only job is to listen and connect."

Hardison likes to quote one of his own clients, Byron Katie, who says, "If you have a problem, you have a solution. There's no problem without a solution."

When Hardison started coaching me a decade ago, fear dominated my life. Especially my professional life. But he was able to connect to me on such a deep level that I knew he had the same fears I had. And his growth to transform fear became my own. His commitment to me was total, and I could feel it in every coaching session. I was no longer alone. I was connected now to the whole universe and all its energy.

I have seen Hardison give so much of himself away in a coaching session that he emerges physically drained to the point of almost not existing.

"It's an exchange of life," he says of coaching that works. "It's almost like giving a blood transfusion. But when the people you coach can see what they're afraid of and then meet it, it's exhilarating!"

Exhilarating financial transformations occur, too. I watched Hardison coach TimeMax from deep debt to exhilarating, staggering profits. I experienced my own professional life go through the same change. His coaching was not just some New Age amateur psychotherapy—it combined the very best of sports coaching and business consulting to produce astonishing quantum leaps in productivity.

Hardison taught me to create from the present moment. He showed me the startling leverage we have in the present-moment actions we take. He taught me to let the past dissolve away. He showed me that my future was just an anxious anticipation. Did I want to spend my whole life swinging between memory and anticipation like a bipolar monkey in a jungle of fear? Or would I like to swing on a star?

To me every hour of the day and night is
an unspeakably perfect miracle.

—Walter Chrysler

Hardison introduced me to Duane Black a few years ago and told me that Duane was one of the few leaders in the corporate world who was fearless about bringing love, nobility, and integrity into the workplace, treating work itself as a sacred act.

I was *very* interested in that. And after meeting with Duane and coproducing seminars and workshops for his leadership teams,

I knew Hardison was right. The extraordinary financial success of the company Duane worked for was no accident.

Duane was genuinely excited about his team of people. And I recalled that Hardison had always told me that most of what is called coaching today is not really effective. There is no commitment to relatedness, and if a "coach" has no excitement about listening to the other person, no change will take place.

After Walter Chrysler had built a dramatically successful automotive company against great odds in the 1940s, he said, "I feel sorry for the person who can't get genuinely excited about his work. Not only will he never be satisfied, but he will never achieve anything worthwhile."

This kind of excitement is not passive or limp. That's a big mistake people make when they first hear about hands-off management. They think it's soft. It's the opposite.

Coaching is about what's possible

Coaching is all about allowing what's possible to emerge. It's moving a person out of being stuck in a mindset where they think they are limited. The coach maintains what the Zen masters call a "beginner's mind" in which nothing is impossible.

Because as an effective coach you never want to seem to be saying "I'm better than you, I'm your superior, and that's why I'm coaching you and telling you how it ought to be." That would be the expert giving advice, not a professional partner delivering coaching. Expert advice will not bring change. It is more likely to bring humiliation. And that's only because we are dealing with human beings.

Lasting behavioral change is always the ironic specialty of the hands-off manager. By not micromanaging, more things change. By keeping your hands off the process, the process improves more quickly.

Would you pull a flower up from the ground with your hands to help it grow?

Why try to do similar things to an employee?

When you are listening to somebody, completely, attentively, then you are listening not only to the words, but also to the feeling of what is being conveyed, to the whole of it, not part of it.

—Jiddu Krishnamurti

The hands-off manager has the added benefit of time. She is not spending all of her time looking over the shoulders of her employees. She has hired good people, she is passionate about what her company is up to, so her people feel inspired. She addresses problems as they occur.

She uses this time to stay up to speed on market trends, to monitor the market, to move her people in strategic ways that anticipate what is coming next. She has a clear mind and can access new ideas easily. The market is always changing. In today's world, those changes can be dramatic and devastating to those who will not listen to the marketplace.

Listening to the marketplace is as important as listening to your people. A true leader and manager simply must have a sense of what is ahead and be prepared to change to address it. If you don't, your organization has little hope of withstanding the test of time.

A salesperson we knew named Trina was down on herself for not making enough cold calls during the day. She said, "I just need to prospect more. I don't do enough prospecting. I know that's my greatest flaw, I don't enjoy it and I put it off and handle things that I think are more important, and then the prospecting never gets done."

"Great. So how does that look to you when you come to work?"

(We asked that because we really wanted to see how prospecting looked to Trina. Why it looked a little scary, unpleasant, and uncomfortable, and why the other work Trina did looked really fun and enjoyable. A coach seeks to understand how a thinking system—"this is the fun part, this is the not fun part"—is leading to low performance. In fact, it's guaranteeing it.)

When we were with Trina for a while in the coaching session, we had a few breakthroughs. She began to see that if she were to create an interesting routine for cold calling, she wouldn't have to try to decide whether she "felt like" doing it. She would simply follow her routine. She wouldn't have to feel that pit in her stomach as she drove to work, wondering if she was going to be able to get herself to prospect. She would now have a rather fun routine to cover that for her.

A system at play in every workplace

In the uncoached, micromanaged organization there is an unconscious default system of judgment and reprimand.

We learned it in families when we were growing up. We surely learned it in the military. Most people in American corporations default unconsciously to a 1940s system of military management combined in some unhealthy way with parent-child discipline.

And hands-off coaching is the way out of that.

Because hands-off coaching is a mature partnership— two grown-ups with a common goal—not Mad Dad criticizing Bad Child (how most teams are run).

A great coach is more committed to the success of the team than he is to the success of any individual. So his mission when coaching his people is to show them that success comes from what they can contribute to the whole, not from how they can stand out as individuals. And this allows him to apply some very tough love to the individual in the name of the team win.

"The hands-off manager has to be absolute," says Duane. "He or she can't be wishy-washy when it comes to excellence. There must be an unwavering commitment to everyone becoming the best they can be at what they do."

And these results are not numbers or money (although they will be nice side effects, in the long run). These results are the ever-improving quality of work. They are the process of great work, not just the financial outcome.

Know when to fold 'em

A coach with true commitment to the vision can light you up even when he's fictional! My wife, Kathy, was working for a large organization whose leader was taking hands-off to a negative extreme. It was no-hands-at-all, no head, no heart, no leadership, no direction, and no vision. Kathy hadn't figured out exactly what felt so wrong at work each day, but she knew she didn't like it.

Then one afternoon she and I went to a movie called *Any Given Sunday* with Al Pacino playing the head football coach of a team in disarray. In one brilliantly dramatic scene, Pacino calls his team together in the locker room and allows himself to burst like a fountain of passion and fire. He pours his heart out on the subject of team and the beauty of all-for-one and one-for-all.

In the movie, Pacino's team—like Kathy's team at work—had become demoralized. There were jealousies, politics, and drama going on all day instead of a single unified mission.

"We're in hell!" Pacino yelled to his team in the locker room before the final game of the season. "Either we heal as a team or we crumble. But we can heal. We can fight our way back into the light...we can climb out of hell one inch at a time. What will it be? Look into the eyes of the person next to you. Either we heal now—as a team—or we will die as individuals."

Kathy was in tears. She knew right then and there what was missing in the company she worked for. And she knew the missing leader wasn't just going to appear. There was no Al Pacino to pull them all back into a team.

When she went to work the following Monday, she put in her two-week notice and hit the pavement looking for other work.

The next company she worked for had true leadership at the top and was a joy to work for. And had it not been for Pacino in *Any Given Sunday* she may never have seen the higher vision.

The main ingredient in stardom is the rest of the team.

—John Wooden

If it's not fun, you're not doing it right

The hands-off coach knows to link mastery to enjoyment. There's always a component of greater enjoyment when people get good at what they do. Notice when you watch a golf match and you see a golfer enjoying the process. A spring in his step, a twinkle in his eye. Playing to win.

The person with fear is always playing not to lose

Great coaching takes the fear out of the workplace. That's one of the vital things the legendary business efficiency guru Dr. W. Edwards Deming preached to the companies he transformed: Whatever you've got going on, you must take the fear out of the system, because that will always sabotage the system.

Should you fire someone for being afraid? Or for being unhappy? Wow. That sounds like the ultimate cruelty. They are already unhappy and now you're going to fire them?

It reminds me of British philosopher Colin Wilson's observation that the fastest, most efficient way to change the mental state of a depressed person is to throw him down a flight of stairs. Depression wouldn't be there anymore. It would certainly be replaced by something else.

Although Wilson was being deliberately absurd and insensitive, his point was well-taken.

Unhappy people don't make as much money as happy people (when everything else is equal). They don't produce or perform as well in the workplace, either. So, yes, it is your role as coach to address the issue and solve it.

Many corporate cultures almost guarantee widespread unhappiness by being conditioned to be fearful of criticism "from above." Soon everyone is living in paranoia, hoping nothing "goes wrong" today.

The hands-off manager cultivates a culture of NO FEAR. Teammates can be bold *and* happy. They can make mistakes and "fail forward."

A woman named Stella who owned a home design business recently sat down with me for some coaching. She wanted to know what to do about Rosie, one of her veteran employees, who came to work angry every day.

"Every day?" I asked. "She comes in angry every day?"

"Every day."

"Why does she still work for you?" I asked.

Stella looked stunned. She was taken aback by my question. Which was the reaction I was hoping for.

I pressed her further. "Does her anger affect your other employees?" I asked.

"Yes, of course. It makes them very uncomfortable."

"Every day?"

"Just about, yes."

"And what about you? Does her anger—the anger she brings into work—does it infect or affect your own mental well-being?"

"All the time. That's why I called you."

"So let's look at it logically," I said. "Business—when it succeeds—is logical. When it fails, it's emotional."

"Okay," she said.

"What if this person—this Rosie—came into work and sprayed an aerosol can of skunk mist throughout your showroom and offices every day. What would you do?"

"I'd tell her to stop. And if she did it again, I'd dismiss her."

"But why?"

"Because she would be damaging our ability to do business."

"And she's not now?"

Stella grew very quiet. Finally, she started nodding her head.

"So I just fire her for being angry?"

"No, you coach her. First you see if you can help her find herself so she can be happy and very proud of her work."

"And if she refuses?"

"You decide what's next. But don't leave it like this. Remember, nowhere is it written that you have to put up with unhappy or angry people. It's not in the Bill of Rights."

Stella was even tougher than I expected her to be. The next day that Rosie showed up angry and cursing, Stella sent her home and told her to take a paid week off, and when she came back next week they would talk about her future with the organization.

Rosie was stunned, shocked, and a little frightened. She had just been thrown down a flight of stairs.

The hands-off manager is not a coward.

The ultimate level of coaching

Are you willing to take a risk? Are you willing to coach from outside the norm, and make a dramatic swing in your thinking?

We have discussed two types of coaches thus far. One is the mentor within the organization, the other is an outside consultant, as I am. Both types of coaching can have a dramatic effect on your people if you will use them.

There is a third approach that incorporates both of the first two but at a much different level. It cannot even begin to be executed by an old-school hands-on manager or micromanager. So if you cannot give that up, do not attempt to go to this level; it will not serve you.

I will call this level "Coaching so you are no longer needed." Many managers are afraid of this very thought. They are so attached to their insecurities and egos that it's the last frontier they want to travel to. But if they could get there, it would reveal its astonishing power.

What if your goal with everyone on your team was to help them find such greatness within themselves that they no longer needed you to oversee their work?

The first step in this process is to shift your worried mind. You must give up the limiting belief that your people are inherently weak or lazy. Those deficiencies only exist when people let their fears interfere with their potential. So your biggest job becomes replacing fear with love in the hearts of those who work for you.

We have talked about tough love in this chapter and it may seem contradictory to see how that idea combines with "replacing fear with love." But they go together. And that just might be because they are both in alignment with mother nature.

Nature, like a good coach, is selective. If you are not prepared when you venture into the desert without water, you will not survive. Does this mean that nature is cruel? Hardly. It means that nature is honest! Nature is reality. Plants and animals give their lives that we might survive and prosper, but we as managers do not want to honor the same universal system with our people.

We want to promote someone to a higher position because we like them. Or because we owe them a favor, or because we don't want to disappoint them. The rationales are endless. But the practices are unnatural. Nature would never do this "for" you. And yet nature has created the most beautiful world that anyone can imagine.

Nature gives its offspring everything it has. Nothing is withheld. And yet if you do not get in harmony with it, you will not be allowed to continue in its presence. The response is sometimes slow, so we imagine that we have escaped the consequences of the law of nature when we have not. If we continue to use oil the way we do now, one day we will have no more oil. If we over-fertilize our fields, one day they will no longer produce a harvest. If we continue to pollute our air, one day we will no longer be able to breathe without becoming ill. Nature is absolute in its commitment to sustainability. Nature will always ultimately choose the good of the whole over the good of the individual.

But will you?

We sometimes think we are getting ahead when we compromise the well-being of another in order to gain something for ourselves. We rationalize this by calling it capitalism or competition. Yet what is more truly competitive than nature itself? One species is always sacrificing in an effort to facilitate a stronger one to prosper. This is not harsh. This is real beauty unfolding. Is it harsh that a tree provides so much shade that grass will not grow below it? Is it harsh that plants will not grow without water? Is it harsh that we cannot survive without food? No, it is beautiful because it is the way of nature. As truly hands-off managers, we understand this principle. We will not choose something for ourselves if it is going to compromise the well-being of the whole. We realize that the best thing we can do for ourselves is to do what is best for the whole.

Hands-off management decisions reflect this understanding. We do not make choices from fear, we make choices from love—a love of what works, not of what we wish would work.

This is what a sports coach does when he doesn't move his friend's son to first string just because he likes him more. This is what a coach does when he releases a player who is no longer contributing to the success of the team. This is not cruel, this is real love—a love of what follows the natural way.

Now for the next level: A true leader does not try to instill a need in his people for more and more of his leading. He shows them how they can lead themselves. A true coach does not believe that his people lack ability. He knows that everyone has life in them and that the potential of life is unlimited. He understands that this is a whole system and some people are better doctors than lawyers. Some are better accountants than artists. Everyone has a gift—a greatness within them wanting to come out and be discovered. He sees everyone as amazing and incredible, yet different.

The hands-off manager's job is to align her employee's gifts with what they are being asked to contribute. When this task is complete, the manager's final, ultimate job is revealed: She gives her employees to themselves. She steps aside and lets them become their own coaches. She knows her wisdom can't compete with the greatness of life that is within them. She understands that they are now aligned with who they are and ready to be on their own. They have "grown up." She surrenders her position as coach. Now their fullest potential can be fulfilled. Now their true nature, their highest selves, the highest possibilities, have the invitation and the freedom to emerge.

This coach's new role is to remind her employees of this when they forget, and provide them with all of the back-up, tools, equipment, and manpower they need to be successful. The hands-off manager is now functioning more like a fellow employee than a boss!

Steps to hands-off success in your life

Three action steps to take after reading this chapter.

1. If you see yourself as a manager, supervisor, and leader only, make the commitment today to be a coach, mentor, and partner instead.

2. If your company employs outside coaching for its executives and top account people (most companies do), ask to get some coaching from one of them. It will give you experience receiving coaching from a pro, and you can use that experience to learn how to coach others.

3. Ask someone in your organization to coach you on something today. Sit with them and take notes. Notice how good it feels to be completely open to coaching.

Work is love made visible.

—Kahlil Gibran

RECOMMENDED READING

Duane Black

Good to Great by Jim Collins
Servant Leadership by Robert Greenleaf
Built to Last by Jim Collins and Jerry Porras
Leading Quietly by Joseph Badaracco

Steve Chandler

Circle of Innovation by Tom Peters
Work and Money by Byron Katie
Loving What Is by Byron Katie
Conscious Business by Fred Kofman

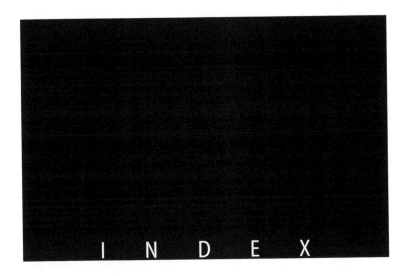

INDEX

ABOUT THE AUTHORS

Steve Chandler is one of America's best-selling authors. His 16 books have been translated into more than 20 languages throughout Europe, China, Japan, the Middle East, and Latin America. His first audiobook, *100 Ways to Motivate Yourself,* was named as *Chicago Tribune*'s Audiobook of the Year in 1997, and King Features Syndicate repeated the honor by naming Chandler's *50 Ways to Create Great Relationships* the 1999 Audiobook of the Year.

Chandler is a business coach and world-famous public speaker who was once called by Fred Knipe, a four-time Emmy award-winning PBS screenwriter, "an insane combination of Anthony Robbins and Jerry Seinfeld." He recently starred in an episode of NBC's *Starting Over*, the Emmy-award winning reality show about life-coaching.

Chandler has been a trainer and consultant to more than 30 Fortune 500 companies worldwide. He graduated from the University of Arizona with a degree in creative writing and political science, spent four years in the U.S. Army in language and psychological warfare, and has been a guest faculty lecturer at the University of Santa Monica, where he teaches in the graduate program of soul-centered leadership.

You can read Steve Chandler's blog at his Website, *www.stevechandler.com*, and contact him via e-mail at stephendchandler @cs.com. You can subscribe to Chandler's motivational messages at *www.imindshift.com*.

Duane Black is the former executive vice president and chief operating officer of SunCor Development Company, responsible for new acquisitions, legal, accounting, finance, home-building, IT, and community development. He oversaw approximately 150 employees and was a steward of more than 150,000 acres of current and future housing developments in Utah, New Mexico, Arizona, and Idaho.

Born in Monticello, Utah, in 1952, Black is the youngest of eight children of older conservative parents who lived through the depression years. He moved to Mesa, Arizona, in 1965, graduated from Mesa High in 1970. After two years of community college, became an electrician at age 20, a self-employed electrical contractor at 21, a self-employed custom home builder at 24, and a self-employed land developer at 31.

Black went to work for SunCor in 1989 during the real estate economic transition of the Resolution Trust Corporation years, when the government rescued so many failed savings and loans. He became a corporate officer in 1990. He grew his division of the company from a land steward, to a developer, to a home-builder, to a builder of communities.

Black's division was the premier builder of master planned communities in the intermountain west in quality-of-life mid-sized communities, with $250,000,000 in sales annually and more than $30 million a year in net profit.

Duane is now retired and spends most of his time in his mountain home in northern Arizona. His personal interests include philosophy, personal growth, business management, writing, public speaking, golf, flying, and making a difference wherever and whenever possible in people's lives.

Also by Steve Chandler

RelationShift (With Michael Bassoff)

100 Ways to Motivate Yourself

Reinventing Yourself

50 Ways to Create Great Relationships

The Joy of Selling

17 Lies That Are Holding You Back

100 Ways to Motivate Others (With Scott Richardson)

Ten Commitments to Your Success

The Small Business Millionaire (With Sam Beckford)

Two Guys Read Moby Dick (With Terrrence N. Hill)

9 Lies That Are Holding Your Business Back
(With Sam Beckford)

The Story of You

Business Coaching (With Sam Beckford)

Two Guys Read the Obituaries (With Terrence Hill)

100 Ways to Create Wealth (With Sam Beckford)